A Blueprint for Safer Schools

Implementing the Layers of Campus Security

1st Edition
Copyright © 2025
All rights reserved
ISBN: 979-8-9991486-1-2

A Blueprint for Safer Schools
Implementing the Layers of Campus Security

1st Edition
Copyright © 2025
All rights reserved
ISBN: 979-8-9991486-1-2

This publication is designed to provide accurate and authoritative information regarding the subject matter covered. It is sold with the understanding that neither the author nor the publisher is engaged in rendering legal, investment, or accounting services.

While the publisher and author have used their best efforts in preparing this book, they make no representations or warranties with respect to the accuracy or completeness of the contents of this book and specifically disclaim any implied warranties of merchantability or fitness for a particular purpose.

No warranty may be created or extended by sales representatives or written sales materials. The advice and strategies contained herein may not be suitable for your situation. You should consult with a professional when appropriate. Neither the publisher nor the author shall be liable for any loss of profit or any other commercial damages, including but not limited to special, incidental, consequential, personal, or other damages.

The content provided in this publication is for general information purposes only. In no event shall the publisher or the author incur liability for any damages, whether direct, indirect, general, consequential, incidental, exemplary or special, arising from the use of this publication or the information provided herein. The information and materials contained herein including, but not limited to, websites, references, and contact information have been compiled from a variety of sources and, as such, are subject to change without notice.

The recommendations contained in this publication represent the standards of best practices at the time this book was written. Safety and security strategies and local crime trends are dynamic. As the physical conditions and facility usage of the school change and/or are modified, some of the recommendations may change as well. For this reason, security processes must be reviewed and modified to meet the changing needs of the institution.

The publisher and the author have no control over the nature, content, and availability of any of the links and resources referenced herein. The publisher and the author suggest that any entity utilizing this document seeks its own legal review of any plan or program resulting from use of this publication and its content. Use of this publication for advertising or other commercial promotions is prohibited.

Published by Risk Mitigation, LLC.

For inquiries contact the author at:

www.riskmitigationllc.com

Contents

To every school—the heart of our communities.

To the dedicated faculty and staff who work tirelessly to create safe, nurturing spaces for learning and growth.

To the students whose futures we are entrusted to protect, and whose courage and potential inspire us every day.

This book is for you—a commitment to your safety, your well-being, and the promise of a secure place to learn, teach, and thrive.

Foreword

I had the privilege of meeting Bradd Atkinson in 1996, during our time as officers with the Baltimore County Police Department. As a young officer beginning my journey in law enforcement, I could not have predicted that my path would eventually lead me to play a foundational role in school safety at the local, national, and international levels.

As the first School Resource Officer (SRO) in Baltimore County, I established and developed what would become a nationally recognized "Model SRO Agency" under the National Association of School Resource Officers (NASRO). I created and implemented the program's guidelines, protocols, and operations and trained over 5,000 officers from across the U.S. and abroad—including personnel from the Republic of Georgia and South Africa.

Throughout my career, I worked closely with school leaders, law enforcement professionals, federal agencies like the FBI, and government officials. I've authored resources, developed crisis management plans, and served NASRO in various leadership roles, ultimately becoming its first African American board president in 2016.

Looking back, I often wish a book like the one Bradd has written existed during the early stages of my work in school safety. It would have served as a valuable resource—not only for me, but for countless other officers and school leaders working to establish safer learning environments.

Bradd's book presents a clear, actionable framework for building comprehensive school security programs, with an emphasis on fostering a culture of efficacy. He breaks down each component of a successful program in an accessible way, offering school leaders the direction needed to identify and implement effective safety strategies on their campuses.

The work of improving school safety requires dedication, adaptability, and ongoing reflection. This book provides an excellent starting point for that journey and serves as both a guide and a source of inspiration.

Bradd has made a meaningful contribution to the field of school security—and I am proud to support and recommend his work.

— Don Bridges
Retired Baltimore County Police SRO
Former President of the National Association
of School Resource Officers N.A.S.R.O.

Preface

The Author Bradd S. Atkinson is the Founder and President of Risk Mitigation, LLC. a Maryland based consulting firm that provides Safety & Security Assessments, Emergency Operation Plan Development, and a variety of different Emergency Preparedness and Response Training programs to its clients.

Bradd chose to name his company Risk Mitigation because it summarizes the goal of what's desired when establishing, implementing and maintaining a successful Safety and Security Program. The words Risk and Mitigation by definition are summarized as:

Risk—a situation involving exposure to danger and the possibility that something unpleasant or unwelcome will happen.

Mitigation—the effort to reduce loss of life and property by lessening the impact of disasters.

Preface

For over a decade a large part of Bradd's focus has been on school security. He has worked with many schools across the country both public and private. During this time, Bradd has seen a common theme in that many schools are unfamiliar with the best practices of a complete school security program. He understands that in most cases school administrators do not have a background in school security and the knowledge of best practices needed to develop a complete program. He also understands the many challenges schools face each day when it comes to securing their campuses.

Bradd has been driven to develop the knowledge and skills to offer schools the support and services they need to develop their security programs at the highest level and to educate the educators in an area they are often not well-versed in. Going beyond what Bradd offers through his company and services he has felt compelled to offer his knowledge of what's needed to develop a complete modern day school security program by writing a book that can be used as an educational guide to schools everywhere.

Introduction

Every school, whether public or private, rural, or urban, faces a unique set of challenges based on its usage, demographics, terrain, staffing levels, and clientele. There isn't and never will be a one-size-fits-all solution to security regardless of what type of facility or institution you are trying to protect. Integrating safety and security enhancements into an academic setting can be difficult when taking a school's dynamics, culture, and mission into consideration. The goal for any school is to maintain a culture of trust and respect while also providing a safe learning environment for its students, a safe working environment for its employees and giving families the assurance that their loved ones are in a safe place each day.

It's important to point out that a complete School Security Program consists of many layers. I often compare these layers to a Smith Island Cake. For those who are not familiar with a Smith Island Cake it's the State of Maryland's official dessert. The cake consists of eight to ten thin layers of yellow cake with chocolate frosting between each layer. The point is that just one, two or even three layers does not make a Smith Island Cake, its many layers that all work together in combination to make the cake complete.

A complete school safety and security program should include the proper use of physical structures and landscapes, the integration of hardware and software technologies, the use of appropriate policies and procedures and the use of people who are ready to respond.

Regularly training every employee on emergency response procedures will give your staff the confidence they need to act quickly when a crisis occurs. Doing this will keep both them and your students safer and decrease the chances that someone will get hurt during the response.

Additionally, the formation and utilization of specialized teams consisting of diverse groups of school employees is also very important. Having specialized teams such as Response Teams, Threat Assessment Teams, Incident Command Teams, and Campus Watch Teams will allow for a more advanced response and effective crisis management from each specific team.

Training each team with content specific to their duty and role gives team members the confidence and empowerment they need to fill their position on the team. Security guards, whether they are in house, contracted, unarmed or armed can also be an effective layer of protection that is detailed later in the book.

Although developing a complete security program may seem like a daunting task, when given the proper guidance and support is much easier than most would think. It is a process that does require some time and effort but once established it is invaluable.

Introduction

In the world of emergency management hope is not a strategy and as I often say, *"It's too late to prepare if it's already happened"*. The following pages will provide you with an oversight of the many aspects of school security and will explain what's required to develop a complete school security program.

Target Hardening is a term that is often used when it comes to Crime Prevention. Enhancing and fortifying Grounds and Buildings has been an effective tactic used for thousands of years to make it more difficult to enter an area and or structure. By definition it's a proactive approach to enhance by fortifying the physical environment and implementing security measures.

"School target hardening" refers to a crime prevention strategy that focuses on making schools more secure by implementing physical security measures and procedures to deter and mitigate potential threats.

Crime Prevention Through Environmental Design, also known as (CPTED) for short, is a multi-disciplinary approach to crime prevention that uses urban and architectural design and the management of built and natural environments. CPTED is pronounced 'sep-ted', and it is also known around the world as Designing Out Crime, Defensible Space, and other similar terms.

CPTED strategies aim to reduce victimization, deter offender decisions that precede criminal acts, and build a sense of community among inhabitants so they can gain territorial control of areas, reduce crime, and minimize fear of crime.

Crime Prevention Through Environmental Design (CPTED) in schools involves strategically designing the physical environment

1

to promote safety, deter crime, and enhance a sense of security for students and staff.

The Key CPTED Principles are as follows:

Natural Surveillance:
Maximizing visibility by strategically placing windows, lighting, and landscaping to allow for clear observation of the school grounds and buildings.

Natural Access Control:
Controlling access points through the use of fencing, landscaping, and signage to make it clear where entry and exit points are.

Territorial Reinforcement:
Defining school property boundaries through landscaping, fencing, and signage to create a sense of ownership and discourage trespass.

Activity Support:
Designing spaces to promote positive activities and discourage potentially problematic behaviors, such as ensuring that drop-off and pick-up areas are well-lit and visible.

Maintenance:
Maintaining the school grounds and buildings in good condition, addressing issues like graffiti, broken windows, and overgrown vegetation promptly to prevent the appearance of neglect and deter crime.

The following are all forms of Target Hardening as well as CPTED.

Fences

The primary purpose of fencing school grounds is to clearly identify the boundaries of the property and to notify users that within those boundaries certain behavior is expected.

Fences can also help control access to your campus. Fences can direct vehicle and pedestrian traffic to safer locations that are easily observed as well as to funnel both vehicles and pedestrians to authorized and controlled points of ingress and egress.

Fencing of play areas is desirable in an elementary school setting because it protects children and others from roaming away or into traffic as well as creating an obstacle for trespassers to overcome. In middle or high school settings, property boundaries should be clearly defined, and partial fencing should be used in secluded areas that cannot be easily monitored.

The selection of fencing material should be based upon the use and location of the fence. When possible, fencing should be wrought iron, aluminum, chain link, cable, corral, separated pickets, split rail or other see-through construction. The fence's purpose is to protect, deter, and reveal. A five-to-eight-foot fence is more than adequate to accomplish these goals. Consideration must be given to entry and exit points. Entry locations should be kept at a minimum and located in highly observable areas.

Gates

Campus entrances and property lines are where access control begins. Having the ability to close vehicle access to the campus with a gate can be a deterrent. Gates can be manual or automatic and are available in a variety of styles. Gates can help to restrict unauthorized access of pedestrian and vehicle traffic to school property during evenings, weekends and holidays.

Gates should be made of material equal to or better in quality than fencing with special consideration given to the latches or locks if used. If a fenced area must be locked, the type of lock that is used must be in compliance with applicable local building and fire codes for egress, meaning although the gate may lock from the outside it needs to be easily opened from the inside to allow people to exit the area quickly.

Every effort should be made by school security officials and or maintenance personnel to patrol the area daily to ensure that all gate hardware is functioning properly.

Trees and Shrubs

Trees, plants, and shrubbery may be just as effective as fencing materials when used to clearly identify school boundaries. The presence or absence of vegetation is a clear indicator of the desired or undesired use of an area. Worn trails indicate cut-through paths of use and should be addressed by legitimizing the cut-through either by placement of a sidewalk or designated paths or eliminating the cut-through.

Trees and shrubs serve many purposes and are desirable. However, if not maintained properly, they may become sources of concealment or an area to hide criminal activity. Proper sight lines should be maintained when pruning trees, shrubs and plants to ensure that concealment areas are eliminated.

Trees should be trimmed from the ground up to the first branch at a height of no less than eight feet. The closest branch should be at least ten feet from a building. Tree canopies should not block illumination from installed lights. Shrubs should be trimmed to a maximum of three feet in height, particularly shrubs in close proximity to windows and doors. Regular pruning to maintain proper sight lines will ensure that routine patrols and bystanders have the opportunity to view and report suspicious activity.

Exterior Lighting

Exterior lighting is essential in the education sector. Light illuminates the school grounds, helping to keep students, faculty and visitors safe. For schools that are located near homes and neighborhoods outdoor lighting can also provide added security for nearby neighbors.

Modern technology such as advanced LEDs and lighting controls is making it easier for schools to reduce their energy usage and be cost-effective while still keeping the campus illuminated.

Campus size and design vary, along with external structures. Pathways, parking lots, lecture halls, and sports facilities all have different outdoor lighting requirements. Outdoor lighting should ensure that all entrances, pathways and parking areas are illuminated.

Larger campuses require more lighting to cover parking lots, multiple entrances, and perimeter illumination. Installing lighting controls reduces energy usage on large campuses. The controls automatically dim or turn off the lights when the space isn't in use.

Switching to LED lighting will bring additional energy savings as well.

Proper lighting is necessary for people to see and be seen and can have a substantial impact on reducing crime. Lighting should allow the identification of a face from approximately 30 feet for someone with normal vision.

Motion sensor enabled lighting can work in conjunction with security cameras to help prevent vandalism and identify offenders. Motion sensors also reduce light trespass and lower energy usage by only turning the lights on when movement is detected.

All exterior lights should be included in your daily routine campus inspection list to ensure they are in working order.

Property Entrance Signage

The primary point of entry to every campus should be easily identifiable by use of signage that can be easily seen and identified by the public. If there is more than one entry point or other access points used for emergency entry or exit, then these areas should also utilize signage indicating their purpose. The school's address should also be present at all the entry points to campus.

For effective school entry signage, prioritize clear and concise messaging, using large, legible fonts and high-contrast colors, and ensure that signs are strategically placed for visibility and accessibility, especially for those with disabilities. You should also ensure that your signage is legible from a distance, especially for those entering the school campus. Easily identified signage is critical not only for visitors but also for first responders when locating your campus while responding to a call for service.

Property Boundary Signage

Signage can also serve to identify property markers and boundaries. Place your signage at eye level so it is easily visible and accessible to all and be sure to position it in well-lit areas avoiding places where shadows or dimly lit areas are. Strategic placement of signage can be useful for wayfinding to guide visitors and students to the right locations, such as the office or specific classrooms. Use universal symbols that are internationally recognized symbols for safety and accessibility. You should also ensure signage is accessible to people with disabilities, following ADA guidelines and mark all special and designated entrances and exits clearly for safety and security.

Entrance Door Signage

Clear signage that directs legitimate visitors to the proper entry points serves the dual role of controlling access and providing notice of prohibited behavior.

The primary point of entry should be easily identifiable by design and the use of signage indicating it as the public entrance. Each additional door should be secured to prevent entry and allow emergency exit only through use of exit/panic bar hardware.

To control admittance, it is recommended that only one entrance to each building be designated for public access. On the exterior of all doors not designated as the main entrance, signage should be posted that directs all visitors to the main entrance and states that they must report to the office. For example, "All visitors must enter through the main entrance and report to the office."

Emergency Signage

Placing "Emergency" signage throughout the campus can serve many purposes. These signs should be highly visible and meet specific regulatory standards to comply with local and state laws. In addition to general safety signs, schools should also include specific directional signs that indicate handicap accessible areas, first-aid stations, and emergency equipment throughout campus.

The use of campus signs that provide emergency numbers can also be beneficial for those who need to contact security or maintenance to report an issue. Signage can also be customized with school branding, but this branding should not interfere with the signs intent of being clearly visible. The use of emergency campus signage can also prove useful for visitors who are on campus after-hours and weekends.

The use of number signage to label building windows and doors is in accordance with accepted practices from the Incident Command System. When emergencies occur, the rapid response of emergency responders to the incident can be critical. During an emergency it may be necessary for responders to gain access through the door or window closest to the emergency scene.

- Doors and windows should be labeled on the exterior with numbers that are in numerical order starting with the main entrance in a clockwise direction and should be visible from a distance of at least 50'.

- Like doors, all windows should be identified from the exterior with corresponding classroom numbers that are large and visible to aid in an emergency response.

Having your building's windows and doors labeled with consistent signage for emergencies is a very good addition that will allow first responders the ability to quickly identify the best possible point of entry in reference to the location of an emergency. This greatly reduces the response time of emergency responders when they are trying to navigate their way into your building.

In addition, I recommend developing a building floor plan that identifies all numbered doors and windows. This emergency map should be kept inside "Go Kits" with multiple copies for use in a potential emergency.

Signage Maintenance and Material

Regularly inspect and maintain signs to ensure signs are clean, legible, and in good condition. Update signs as needed by keeping information current and relevant., and finally, you should consider using durable materials that can withstand weather and wear and tear over time.

Exterior Doors and Door Hardware

All door systems for schools should meet the minimum requirements set forth for commercial establishments. Exterior doors should be constructed in a metal frame of steel, aluminum alloy, or solid hardwood core. All windows should be tempered safety glass or polycarbonate sheeting.

Any exposed hinges should be of the non-removable pin hinge type. Minimum one-hour burn rated fire doors should be installed where specified by fire code such as in stairwells. All doors should also be equipped with hardware that prevents chaining or barring the doors from within or without.

Protocols for the janitorial staff, maintenance staff and security staff to ensure that the campus is fully locked by a certain time each day after school should be in place and enforced by the administration. The protocol should include a daily routine checklist of all exterior doors and windows to ensure that every exterior door and window is working properly and has been closed and secured at the end of the day upon closure.

Exterior Windows

To provide maximum surveillance of walkways, courtyards, and school grounds, all exterior windows should remain uncovered by papers, blinds, and drapes. Windows in a school environment should use glazing that is scratchproof lexan, polycarbonate, or other break resistant coated material. All glazing should be in good condition, free from cracks and/or breaks.

All ground level windows should have functioning latches capable of securing the window and not being easily defeated. It is recommended that all basement/ground level windows be secured with additional security measures. Windows designed for emergency escape should not be difficult to open from the inside or blocked by screens.

Protocols for the janitorial staff, maintenance staff and security staff to ensure that the campus is fully locked by a certain time

Classroom doors should have a mechanism that allows teachers to lock the door from inside without opening it, minimizing exposure to potential threats in the hallway. Door locks that do not require the use of a key are preferred for ease of use during emergency situations that require the door to be locked quickly and easily.

The use of a lever style deadbolt is recommended due to its simplicity. The inside lever should always remain unlocked to ensure easy and quick exit in case of emergencies. Authorized personnel (administrators, security, first responders) should have access to unlock the door from the outside, either with a key or another credential.

All door hardware should be UL-listed for safety compliance, which tests strength, corrosion, and operation. The height of the lock and latch must be within reach for anyone with a physical handicap, which means it must sit between 15 and 48 inches from the floor.

Locks should also have visual indicators to show occupants the status of the door (locked or unlocked). In addition to the words locked and unlocked many of these types of locks also have green (unlocked) and red (locked) indicators to eliminate confusion.

High Risk Classrooms and Areas

Areas identified as high risk are usually the target of burglaries or accidents. Such high-risk areas may include but are not limited to science rooms/lab, computer lab, music room and other areas in which valuable and dangerous equipment is stored.

These areas should be connected to a quality security alarm system that is monitored by a central monitoring company and local law enforcement. It is recommended that the computer lab, audio visual closet, and other areas associated with high dollar equipment not be marked with signage identifying them but rather identified by room number only.

Areas in which student files are stored, such as counseling offices and main offices, should be alarmed and equipped with high security locks, as rated by the Underwriters Laboratory, U.L.

Cafeterias and Kitchens

The cafeteria is one of the most frequent sites of spontaneous violence. It is often an overcrowded common area where peers may encourage fighting or confrontations. Areas that create a line "bottle neck" effect can contribute to confrontations also.

Avoid overcrowding seating areas and ensure there is ample space between tables. All egress points and doors should also be clear of obstructions to allow for a quick evacuation if necessary.

All exterior cafeteria doors should be kept closed and secured at all times to prevent unauthorized access. Monitoring the cafeteria by utilizing surveillance systems (cameras) and staff presence to identify potential threats and issues can be an effective measure.

Keeping the kitchen area secure should also be a priority due to the risk of injury. Keep all knives locked in a drawer or cabinet when not in use to prevent them from being used as a weapon or for self-harm.

Frequent deliveries to the cafeteria kitchen may necessitate consideration. The visitor policy for this area may need to be adjusted, or cafeteria deliveries excluded from the visitor policy if cafeteria staff directly supervises delivery personnel. All walk-in refrigerator units should be equipped with hardware to open from the inside as well as the outside.

Auditoriums

High occupancy spaces such as auditoriums and theaters should be locked when not in use. They should also be checked before and after they are occupied for an event. These areas are potentially vulnerable to attack due to their ability to hold large numbers of people in an open space.

When these areas are in use during non-school day activities you should restrict access to the rest of the building. This can be accomplished by locking internal doors and or gates in corridors that lead to these areas. Check with your local fire department to ensure doing so doesn't violate fire code and emergency egress.

Custodial Closets and Mechanical Rooms

Students seeking private locations to conduct illicit activities may seek doors known to be open and rooms that are not regularly occupied such as custodial closets and mechanical rooms. These areas not only provide a place for illicit behavior they also present a risk for injury due to students having access to dangerous chemicals, electrical panels and other building systems that may present a hazard. Ensuring these areas are properly posted with the appropriate signage as well as keeping them locked at all times will prevent such things from occurring.

Exterior Utilities

Exterior utilities such as water, gas and electricity should be protected by enclosures to prevent unauthorized access or damage. All valves and panels should be locked to prevent unauthorized access and illicit activity. All air handling systems that provide internal building air should be protected by enclosures that can be locked to prevent someone from introducing dangerous foreign substances into the system.

Please note that if these areas are adjacent to a building and there is a building door within an area that is enclosed by a fence and a gate the gate should allow for emergency egress for individuals exiting the building in emergency situations. In addition, all external gas meters and electrical boxes that would be at risk of being struck by a vehicle should also be protected by bollards.

Scheduled Maintenance

Equipment failure (e.g., burned out light bulbs, broken locks, exposed wiring, etc.) may lead to theft and injury. It is essential that all equipment be inspected and repaired regularly to avoid such mishaps.

As mentioned previously all fencing and gates should be regularly inspected and maintained to ensure they are intact and function properly. Trees, shrubbery and brush that border fences should be trimmed back to prevent them from growing into or over the fence line.

All doors and windows should also be inspected on a regular basis to ensure they are opening, closing and locking properly. Automatic closing mechanisms should be inspected regularly, especially during seasonal temperature changes.

Changes in temperature and humidity can affect a door or windows ability to open and close due to materials expanding and contracting. This can also cause automatic door closures to stick and or hang up in an open position. This problem is often overlooked and unnoticed resulting in open doors.

Establishing a daily checklist for faulty, broken, and routine maintenance items as mentioned and assigning someone to complete it each day can prevent issues from going unnoticed and compromise the safety and security of your campus.

Access control to school campuses and buildings is a top concern for most school officials. Schools often struggle with maintaining a balance between having a friendly, welcoming school climate and a facility which is secure from unwanted intruders.

While even the best school access control efforts will likely not guarantee that a determined outsider will not be able to gain access to the school, educators must take reasonable steps to reduce the risks of unauthorized access.

Main Entrance / Lobby's

All schools should require that visitors enter at one designated entrance. All doors other than the designated entrance door should be secured and treated as exit doors only. A Schools main entrance design should ensure that visual observation of all visitors occurs before they proceed further into the building. By ensuring that the main entrance is visible from the main office or reception area, natural surveillance of the entrance can be achieved, and visitors will also recognize that they are being monitored upon entry.

The check in / screening process should also occur upon the visitor entering the building at the main office or reception area which should be located just inside of the main entrance. A physical barrier, such as a counter or desk should be utilized where visitors check in and are screened. This counter or desk should be equipped with a panic alarm system that is tied to 911. Panic buttons can provide immediate police dispatch during an emergency and can be installed in strategic locations.

Wearable wireless panic buttons are also available so they can be carried by personnel throughout the building and campus. Regardless of whether a panic button is utilized in a fixed location or in a wireless application these devices garner a quick police response without having to call 911.

The counter or desk should also be equipped with multiple means of communication to include a landline and a two-way radio. This area should also be equipped with a surveillance camera that is monitored. The use of surveillance cameras may have a deterrent effect, but they can also be defeated if camera locations are known or if they are not properly monitored and provide no immediate prevention defense. We will discuss this in further detail later in the surveillance camera section.

The use of a vestibule, otherwise known as a double entry system at the primary entrance, is a preferred method that works by allowing visitors to enter the first entrance, but the secondary entrance remains locked. Once in the vestibule area the visitor is required to sign in and is screened before allowing them entry through the second interior door which allows access to the building. As an added layer of security some schools also choose to keep the exterior door to this area locked and require the visitor to use a call button or ai phone before allowing them access into the vestibule area.

To add yet another layer of deterrence to achieve visitor compliance there are schools who also post signage on the exterior of their entry doors and throughout their campus's advising that individuals who do not follow visitation procedures may be charged with criminal trespassing.

Access Control Systems

An access control system is a series of devices to control access among visitors and employees within a facility. It typically works through centralized control via a software interface. Each employee is provided with a level of security so that they are given access to the areas that are needed for them to perform their job functions and restricted access to other areas that they do not need access to.

The central control can vary from a central computer running the software, or a cloud-based system with access from a web browser or mobile phone app. Some systems support integration with other devices for other protections, such as security cameras, break in alarms, carbon dioxide detectors, and smoke and fire detectors.

There are several types of readers and scanning systems that are commonly used at points of entry which we will now discuss below.

Access Cards / Fob Readers

Access Card / Fob Reader access control systems are amongst one of the most popular systems installed on doors to restrict, control and monitor who has entered a building with typically each doorway protected by a card reader. Access cards are provided to authorized users to allow entry once the reader reads their card or key fob. A common configuration is to have some type of card reader to control each doorway. Each person that has access to the facility is then issued a card which gets scanned for access.

These systems are programable and allow the system administrator the ability to grant specific access privileges to each card to include time of day, days of the week, and specific door access. Having these capabilities allows schools to grant different access privileges to their employees. For example, maintenance staff are often given 24-hour 7 day a week access where teachers are given Monday through Friday open to close access. Access cards can also and should be deactivated when an employee is suspended, terminated or is on extended leave.

Certain visitors such as contractors can also be given access cards that can be programed to give them access only to specific areas in the building where they need to perform their duties. These cards can also be programed to allow access during a specific time period and have an expiration date.

There are, however, several things to consider with a card reader system. First is that someone must be responsible for managing the system on a daily basis. This includes issuing temporary cards to contractors, auditing the system on a regular basis to prevent card/fob duplicates as well as managing card deactivation for employees who no longer work there or whose access privileges are temporarily taken away pending an investigation and or suspension.

Second is that people will inevitably lose and misplace cards/fobs, and this requires someone to reprint/re-issue them a new one which requires time and the expense of a new card which many choose to pass onto the employee who lost their card.

Third is that when cards/fobs get lost, they can wind up in the hands of those who should not have access before you realize the card is lost and deactivate it. For this reason, consideration must be taken when deciding whether to issue non-descript cards that are plain with no employee pictures and or entity identifiers such as school names, logos and addresses or cards that double as employee ID cards as well as access cards.

Access Keypads

Access keypads are different than access cards and fobs in that instead of scanning a card on a card reader, you punch in a code on a numeric keypad. For the door to open, you must enter the correct passcode. Keypads are sometimes used instead of card readers, and sometimes in conjunction with card readers.

There are of course advantages and disadvantages to this system as well. The advantage is that you do not have to issue physical cards/fobs which saves time and the expense of the cards/fobs. The disadvantage is that the numeric code can be given to individuals who should not have access.

Biometrics

Unlike access cards, fobs and keypads biometric access control systems use a person's physical traits such as their fingerprints, face, palm and iris. For the door to open you must scan the specified body part on the scanner and it must match your biometric data that is stored in the system. These traits cannot be copied, which increases the accuracy of identification and authentication.

These types of systems are commonly used in high level security commercial and government buildings with adult employees. In a school setting these types of systems can be met with parental resistance due to privacy issues. Meaning parents often do not want their child's physical profiles being taken and stored in a school's security systems database.

Video Intercom Systems

An IP video intercom system can be a valuable tool for enhancing access control methods. These systems offer features like two-way audio, video identification, and remote door release which allow staff to identify and communicate with visitors at entry points, then remotely grant or deny access. IP video intercom boxes, if placed properly, can provide a camera view of a visitor, enabling staff to verify their identity and verbal intentions before allowing them inside.

IP video intercom boxes are commonly used for visitors and not for employees and students. They should be located on the outside of the building at the main entrance and should screen a visitor while the visitor is still on the exterior of the building.

I do not recommend using these systems as a stand-alone method for access control and I have encountered many schools through the years that are. Although these systems can be a useful tool in enhancing access control security measures they should not be used by themselves as the only screening method before allowing a visitor unrestricted access to a school building.

An example would be, if a video intercom system is used to grant a visitor access by a staff member who is located somewhere else in the building, (they are not sitting just inside the door where the visitor is located) they are limited to just what they can see in the video camera and what they can hear through the intercom.

Using these systems as the first layer of access control is the ideal method of use. If a video intercom is used by a staff member who is sitting at a counter or reception desk just inside the exterior door where the visitor and call box is located, they can use the camera and intercom to visually and audibly screen the visitor before deciding whether to allow them entry into the vestibule or reception area where they are seated.

Burglar Alarm Systems

Burglar alarm systems for schools are designed to detect intrusions and monitor breaches. Systems typically function with a three-step process which includes detection, verification, and notification. These systems commonly use motion sensor alarms and door and window contacts to detect movement. The system then sounds an alarm as soon as it is detected and notifies authorities.

The electrical components and sensors can be further connected to the central system, which can also be tied to cameras that will then focus their attention on the area where the intrusion and breech has occurred and can follow the intruder and their movement once they are inside the building.

Burglar alarms can also use passive infra-red, otherwise known as PIR sensors. These types of sensors scan motion within a wavelength invisible to the human eye.

Areas identified as high risk are usually the target of burglaries. These areas may include, but are not limited to, computer labs, music rooms, maintenance shops and other areas in which valuable equipment is stored.

Building sizes and interior layout can also create difficulty when locating intruders. For these reasons a zoned alarm system is often suggested to track the movement of an intruder. Ideally, the alarm system should also have a battery backup for power failures. At a minimum alarm systems should be tested at least every six months.

Identification Badges

Photo identification badges for students, faculty, and staff are commonly used by schools. Many schools require them to display the badge on the outermost article of clothing while on school property. Photo identification badges are a precaution that some schools are finding necessary to keep unauthorized people from entering facilities as it makes unauthorized people more easily identifiable.

Student photo identification badges are a recommended measure for middle and high school students, even if the student may only be required to display their identification when asked by a faculty or staff member.

Photo ID badges also allow for quick and easy identification of students, staff making it easier to spot anyone who doesn't belong on campus preventing unauthorized entry and enhancing overall security. The presence of ID badges can also deter potential intruders by making it evident that the school is a secure environment. In emergency situations, ID badges can help to quickly identify students and staff during evacuations. Badges can also be equipped with barcode or RFID technology to streamline attendance tracking, making it easier for teachers and administrators to manage attendance.

ID badges can also facilitate communication by helping students and staff to easily recognize each other and learn each other's names. This can improve relationships and create a more welcoming environment thus fostering a sense of community and improving communication.

In addition, ID badges can help ensure that students and staff are where they are supposed to be by tracking movement throughout the school premises if you require students to check in certain places by swiping or scanning their identification cards.

Staff members should be required to turn in their photo ID upon separation from employment. Substitute teachers should be given a separate temporary badge that is unique and numbered. Substitutes should be issued badges on a daily basis and should be required to turn their badge in at the end of each day to a full-time office staff member. All daily substitute badges should be accounted for at the end of each day by an office staff member.

Key Control

Key control in large facilities is a significant problem due to personnel turnover and the addition of new buildings. Schools equipped with a mechanical key system, the use of high security locks (as rated by the Underwriters Laboratory, U.L.) is essential.

Access Control

Implementing a key control policy and an annual inventory of keys is recommended. High security locks require keys that are cut by a specialized vendor, making duplicating or manipulating keys more difficult. All lost or unaccounted keys should require a lock change to prevent unauthorized access.

All keys should be distributed and signed for at the beginning of the school year and then collected at the end of the year. One staff member should be assigned this duty and should be identified by position in the school's emergency operation plan (EOP) for quick access to any needed key, or a master key in an emergency. Access to master and grand master keys should be described in policy and limited to essential personnel who have legitimate need for them. In some cases, individual office or classroom keys may be required.

Only one or two people should have possession of master and grand master keys. Typically, these individuals are given the responsibility of opening and closing the facility each day.

A Knox Box is a secure, exterior-mounted key box that provides first responders, like firefighters and law enforcement, with immediate access to a building during emergencies. Ideally a Knox Box should not only be permanently installed in the building's exterior wall to prevent it from being tampered with, but it should also be wired to the school's burglar alarm system to notify authorities if it were tampered with.

Knox Boxes are typically installed near the primary entry door of a building, and they normally will contain keys, access cards, and sometimes floor plans. Each schools individual Knox Box is keyed to a single master key controlled by the local responding departments.

Deliveries, Vendors and Contractors

Deliveries to schools can come from various vendors ranging from food services to office supply companies. Delivery locations can also vary from the main entrance to the cafeteria. School delivery access control issues arise from the need to balance security with the convenience of deliveries, often leading to challenges like unauthorized access, delays, and potential security breaches.

Allowing deliveries without proper identification or verification can lead to unauthorized individuals entering the school premises. Unmonitored deliveries can pose a security risk, as packages could be tampered with or used for malicious purposes.

A significant portion of data breaches affecting K-12 schools involve vendors. Vendors, if not properly vetted and monitored, could potentially access sensitive student data, leading to privacy violations. Schools must comply with regulations like FERPA (Family Educational Rights and Privacy Act), which restrict the disclosure of personally identifiable information in education records without parental consent. Schools are at risk for lawsuits and financial penalties if they fail to properly protect student data.

Contractor access control issues arise from the practical requirements of construction, maintenance, and other services needing to perform work in areas where access is not normally permitted to the public. Contractors might accidentally or intentionally enter restricted areas, compromising security. This often can lead to challenges in managing access permissions while at the same time ensuring a secure environment.

Companies can vary in their hiring practices when it comes to background investigations and hiring requirements. Many companies have a high turnover rate with employees and are hiring on a regular basis. Often, they place employees into their workforce before the results of a background investigation are even back.

For all the reasons stated above schools at a minimum should use a system to track and verify deliveries, allowing only authorized personnel access to the school and develop and communicate clear procedures for deliveries, including designated drop-off and pick-up areas, and required identification. Schools should also train staff on security protocols and procedures for handling deliveries, including how to identify and address potential security risks.

Schools need to thoroughly vet vendors to ensure they have robust security practices and understand the school's data security requirements. Contracts with vendors should include clear stipulations regarding data security, privacy, and access control policies. Schools should also implement a vendor risk management program to identify, assess, and mitigate potential risks associated with vendor relationships.

Schools should either conduct their own thorough background checks on contractors or require the company that they are using to provide current background check results on their employees to ensure they are trustworthy and reliable.

Schools should also establish clear procedures for contractor access, including registration, badge requirements, limit their working in restricted areas without supervision and only provide them with access to the areas they need to work in for the duration of their work by using restricted access cards. Contractors should also be made to visibly wear a visitor/contractor badge at all times while working in the building.

Ultimately it is the responsibility of the school to handle all these individuals as if they were a typical everyday visitor and be sure to train school staff on access control and visitor management procedures and security protocols.

Food Services

Food Services that are contracted by an outside food service company and not self-operated by the school should be involved and compliant with all school safety and security policies, procedures, and protocols. Members of the food service team should also be included in your emergency preparedness training as well as training in first aid and food allergy best practices.

Frequent deliveries to the cafeteria may necessitate consideration. The visitor policy for this area should be reviewed on a regular basis. Cafeteria delivery personnel should be directly supervised by cafeteria staff at all times while inside the school building.

A topic known as Food Defense has components of access control and is worthy of mentioning in this chapter. The United States Department of Agriculture has a useful document titled Creating your school food defense plan which can be found on their website.

The purpose of this document is to have measures in place to reduce the chances of someone intentionally contaminating the food used in your food service operation to harm children and cause panic, alarm, and distrust in the food supply.

Access Control

A food defense plan will help you identify steps you can take to minimize the risk of intentional contamination or tampering of food products in your school. Having a plan will increase preparedness and will be helpful during emergencies.

Food defense is different from food safety although they are similar in that they both focus on preventing the contamination of food. Food safety prevents the unintentional contamination of food products that can be reasonably anticipated based on the type of food product and how it is prepared.

This knowledge can be used to assist you in developing your School Food Safety Plan based on Hazard Analysis and Critical Control Points (HACCP) Principles. If you choose to develop a plan, be sure to refer to the USDA website and consult these documents for information prior to doing so.

Chapter Three
Visitor Management
"Know who's in your building"

Visitor management in schools is crucial for maintaining a safe and secure environment. Having an established process for signing in, verifying identity and accounting for all visitors will ensure that only authorized individuals are on campus, which helps prevent unauthorized access and potential threats.

Visitor Management Protocol

Regulating access to a school requires sound visitor management procedures. Every school should develop a clear and concise visitor policy that includes the following components:

- Who is allowed to visit: Define who is permitted to enter the school premises, such as parents, guardians, volunteers, contractors, vendors and other authorized personnel.
- Identification Requirements: Specify what identification is required for check-in, such as a driver's license or other government-issued ID.
- Badge Requirements: Make it mandatory for all visitors to wear a visible visitor ID badge throughout their time on campus.
- Restricted Areas: Clearly outline which areas of the school are restricted to visitors.
- Check-in/Check-out Procedures: Establish a clear and

efficient process for visitors to check in and out of the school.

- Purpose of Visit: Require visitors to state the purpose of their visit upon check-in.
- Should the visitor be escorted: Depending on the purpose of their visit and the area they are visiting in the building or on the premises, you should define who should be escorted for the duration of their visit.

To summarize, at a minimum, visitors should not be able to enter the school without registering at the main office. This should require proof of identification and the issuance of a visitor badge.

In addition, most if not all visitors should also be escorted during their visit. As previously mentioned, the process for vendors, maintenance trades (i.e. HVAC, electrical, plumbing, etc.) to include all contractors should be the same.

Visitor management programs should also include prominent signage on all building entrances, visitor parking areas and even parking lot entrances. The bottom line is you should let your visitors know your expectations.

Visitor Management Systems

A web-based visitor management system designed for schools can identify and alert school officials when sex offenders, non-custodial parents, terminated employees and pre identified unwanted individuals attempt to enter the school after presenting their Identification and it being processed through the system. A Visitor Management system offers benefits such as:

- Instant Screening - Each and every visitor is instantly screened against the registered sex offender databases in all fifty states.
- Custom Databases - Can check visitors against custom databases set by each school which can contain custody alerts and/or banned visitors.
- Accurate Records - Can ensure that accurate and reliable records are kept for every visitor that enters the school, every day.
- Efficient Reporting - Can quickly and easily create reports to account for all visitors for reports and attendance tracking purposes during an evacuation.

A web-based visitor management system should include the following:

- Digital Sign-In/Out - Use a digital system for recording visitor information, including name, purpose of visit, and time of entry and exit.
- Visitor Badges - Issue personalized visitor badges with the visitor's name, role, photo, destination, and date and time of entry.
- Background Checks - Integrate the system with databases to conduct background checks on visitors, including sex offender checks and custom banned persons lists.
- Visitor Tracking - Implement a system to track visitor activity within the school, ensuring they are where they are supposed to be.
- Emergency Preparedness - Ensure the system can quickly identify all visitors on campus in case of an emergency, aiding in evacuations and headcounts.

Visitor Management

If you choose to implement a web-based system you should provide staff with thorough training on the visitor management procedures and the use of the system. You should also clearly communicate the visitor policy and procedures to all staff, students, and visitors. Be sure to regularly review and update the visitor management procedures to ensure their effectiveness.

The benefits of having a web-based Visitor Management System include enhanced security, which will help to prevent unauthorized access to the school premises. It will also Improve the safety of students, faculty by tracking and monitoring visitor activity.

A system will also streamline your operations by simplifying the visitor check-in/check-out process, thus freeing up staff time. These systems also offer accurate records of all visitors, which can be critical in case of emergencies and finally having a web-based system will help your school comply with safety regulations and best practice.

Chapter Four
Surveillance
"Omnipresent eyes"

Surveillance cameras provide the ability to monitor many areas at one time. They also serve many purposes when used properly. Surveillance cameras in schools can enhance safety and security by deterring crime, providing evidence for investigations, and facilitating emergency response, ultimately fostering a safer learning environment for students and staff.

Extensive data demonstrates numerous advantages associated with investing in a school security camera system, including the prevention of criminal activities, augmenting the presence of security personnel, and providing crucial evidence in the event of an incident within the school environment.

With modern security cameras, a school can be more proactive with campus safety and security. When schools designate staff members to actively monitor the camera system a school can also know when suspicious activities are happening in real time. Video surveillance also improves emergency response for schools and provides a clear indication that the school values safety.

Having reliable, up-to-date information during an emergency is critical and video security cameras can help provide this. Modern systems improve emergency preparedness by helping schools have the ability to respond to incidents quicker with automatic real-time alerts, easily share live footage with emergency responders and proactively detect suspicious behavior with AI Analytics.

Surveillance

When security cameras are placed in plain sight, they have been shown to reduce criminal activity in that area. Often, when a camera is visible, a person will think twice before committing a crime since the possibility of facing negative legal repercussions increases dramatically with security cameras.

During school hours, knowing who is on your campus is crucial for campus safety. The ability to detect unauthorized visitors is also a valuable benefit of having security cameras. Security cameras make it easier to keep track of students, teachers and visitors and allow you to better understand who should or should not be on school property.

AI features like facial recognition can provide a greater ability to detect unauthorized visitors in real time and improve security. Cameras can also show you where trouble spots are, so you can direct everyone in a safe direction.

School security cameras can also decrease bullying and create safer environments for teachers and students and can prevent escalation by automatically detecting aggressive movement, fights, and bullying in real time. In some instances, teachers can harass students and vice versa.

Harassment can be highly detrimental to a child's well-being and academic development, while false accusations damage a teacher's career and reputation. Having security cameras installed in classrooms or public places provides some objective truth when allegations of harassment occur.

If an incident happens, video footage can provide school administration with accurate information that can support quick investigations to protect victims and provide peace of mind as soon as possible by dealing with incidents accurately and fairly by using objective video evidence to verify or disprove bullying accusations.

The two types of systems are either on-premises (NVR) systems or cloud video surveillance systems. Cloud solutions have modern infrastructure that allows remote access to the security camera system through a PC, laptop, tablet, mobile phone or any other internet connected device.

Video surveillance in schools is legal and common, but if security cameras are installed irresponsibly (i.e., hidden cameras that are not clearly visible, or cameras installed in private locations), it can raise the risk of liability regarding privacy.

School security cameras should never be used in places where privacy is required, such as restrooms, locker rooms, and employee lounges. Schools can still protect these areas with alternatives like motion sensors or vape sensors, which provide insight without infringing on a student or employees right to privacy.

Visitors to the campus should immediately be made aware of a surveillance systems existence through prominent signage that notifies them that their actions on your campus are being monitored and recorded.

Security cameras come in different varieties, including bullet, dome, PTZ, and fisheye. Bullet cameras have durable housing in a barrel-like form factor. Dome cameras have dome-shaped housing that is more discreet than that of bullet cameras. Pan tilt zoom (PTZ) cameras can pan and tilt to change where the camera is facing. Fisheye cameras are dome cameras that capture 360° of footage and provide the maximum amount of camera coverage.

Surveillance

Corner cameras are designed to monitor less-visible areas like hallways and corners, enhancing overall school security by preventing misbehavior and safeguarding students and staff. Multi-sensor cameras provide full coverage of the most expansive areas of schools such as hallways, cafeterias, school yards, and parking lots.

Decisions with camera placement and the type of camera used should be made with the level of risk of the associated areas in mind.

Classrooms and entryways, which are known as high-traffic and frequently used areas, are best monitored by dome or bullet cameras that have a 5MP or greater image sensor. These points of entry benefit from security cameras that are powerful enough to capture faces and human activity with detail and accuracy.

Hallways and corridors are typically long and potentially narrow spaces. Fisheye cameras can capture a panoramic 360° or 180° views of these types of environments.

Gyms, cafeterias, and auditoriums are large, open spaces are best covered by a fisheye security camera. Omnidirectional fisheye cameras allow schools to monitor a massive area with just one camera by providing a complete 360° view of the environment with multiple viewing options, including a tile view and immersive view.

Parking lots, sports fields and playgrounds and other outdoor gathering areas typically benefit from security cameras that have long-distance capabilities and a powerful zoom. These types of cameras are ideal for capturing distant activity with accuracy and for reliable license plate recognition and facial recognition.

Once a surveillance system is installed all cameras should be properly identified and indicated on a building and campus map. Having your system mapped will aide in system management and future upgrades.

Chapter Five
Communication
"With the push of a button"

Having a robust communication system in place is crucial for a school to function effectively each day, ensuring everyone is informed, safe, and can collaborate effectively. This includes informing parents, facilitating communication between teachers and students, and enabling a swift response to emergencies.

Mass Notification Systems

A school mass notification system is a vital safety tool that allows schools to quickly and efficiently alert administrators, staff, parents, and first responders about emergencies, safety drills, and other important information. These systems typically utilize various communication channels like text messages, emails, voice-mails, and even silent override messages on smartphones to ensure timely and effective communication.

A mass notification system in a school is specifically designed for real-time alerts during emergencies, like lockdowns or severe weather. A mass communication system, on the other hand, is broader and can be used for routine announcements, schedule changes, and other general communications. Both can use multiple channels like email, text, and social media, but mass notification systems prioritize speed and urgency in crisis situations.

Mass notification systems provide immediate updates during emergencies, allowing for swift responses and minimizing potential harm. They utilize multiple communication methods to reach everyone, including those with hearing or visual disabilities and some systems also allow for targeted messages to specific groups, like notifying teachers without alerting students.

Many systems integrate with panic buttons or other alerting systems, enabling staff to quickly initiate an emergency alert and some systems can even integrate with existing infrastructure like PA systems, desktop computers, and VoIP phone.

Mass Communication Systems

A school mass communication system is a software technology platform that enables schools to quickly and efficiently send alerts, announcements, and updates to students, staff, and parents. Mass notification systems use various channels like email, SMS text messaging, mobile app push notifications, social media, and even visual and audio displays within the school building.

Many systems offer features such as targeted messaging that allow schools to send messages to specific groups (e.g., a particular grade level, bus route, or sports team) rather than broadcasting to everyone.

These systems are also designed for emergency alerting that allow rapid communication during emergencies such as lockdowns, severe weather warnings, or fire alarms. Some systems can even send automated notifications to local authorities or emergency services, helping to expedite response times.

Communications

Mass Communication Systems are typically easy to use intuitive interfaces that allow administrators to create and send messages quickly and efficiently thus improving communication capabilities. By providing a centralized and reliable way to quickly communicate these systems help ensure that everyone receives important information in a timely manner which ultimately enhances safety. The ability to quickly disseminate information during emergencies is vital for ensuring the safety of students, staff, and the broader school community.

Schools most commonly use mass communications to send messages to staff members, parents and students about school delays or closures due to weather-related events. These systems can also be used to initially alert as well as send updates to students and staff about situations such as severe weather events to warn everyone of incoming storms, tornadoes, or other extreme weather conditions to ensure timely sheltering or evacuation.

They can also be used for active threats to provide immediate alerts about intruders or violence on campus to initiate lockdowns or other safety measures and cyber-attacks to notify stakeholders about data breaches, ensuring swift actions to protect sensitive information.

Mass Communication Systems can also be used as a day-to-day communication tool to maintain operational efficiency and community engagement for things such as announcements to share important updates or reminders to keep the school community informed, service interruptions to communicate disruptions in utilities or IT services, allowing for quick adjustments or troubleshooting, events to promote school activities or meetings to ensure high participation and engagement and celebrations to highlight achievements or milestones, fostering a sense of community and morale.

Mass Notification vs. Mass Communication

A school mass notification system primarily focuses on immediate alerts during emergencies, like active shooter situations or severe weather. It's designed to quickly broadcast crucial information and instructions to the entire campus and potentially to parents and guardians. A school mass communication system, on the other hand, is a broader platform for all school-related announcements and updates, including both emergency alerts and routine information like event reminders or attendance notifications.

As mentioned, a mass notification system in a school is specifically designed for real-time alerts during emergencies, like lockdowns or severe weather. A mass communication system, on the other hand, is a broader platform that can be used for routine announcements, schedule changes, and other general communications. Both can use multiple channels like email, text, and social media, but mass notification systems prioritize speed and urgency in crisis situations.

Below is a summarized comparison between the two.

Mass Notification System:
Purpose: Primarily for emergency situations and immediate alerts.

Focus: Quickly disseminate critical information and instructions during emergencies.

Communications

Examples: Active shooter alerts, lockdown instructions, severe weather warnings.

Channels: May include loudspeakers, voice messages, text messages, email, and push notifications.

Mass Communication System:
Purpose: Broader platform for all school communications, including emergencies and routine updates.

Focus: Facilitates communication between the school, parents, students, and staff.

Examples: Event reminders, attendance notifications, school newsletters, and emergency alerts.

Channels: May include email, text messages, social media, and school websites.

Features: May include two-way communication, personalized messaging, and multilingual options.

In essence, a mass notification system is a subset of a mass communication system. It's the specialized part of the broader system designed for time-sensitive emergency alerts. Both are equally important and should be used in conjunction with each other to cover all the bases of communication.

Redundancy when it comes to communication, especially during emergencies, is vital to ensure that everyone will receive the message in a timely manner regardless of what method of communication they receive it through.

Public Address (P.A.) System

School Public Address Systems are used for operational and emergency communications. PA Systems should have the capability of relaying a message to every building and every room within a building throughout campus.

These systems should also be able to relay messages to all external areas of the campus utilizing external speakers that are loud enough to be herd by everyone. Highly used areas to include all sidewalks, pathways, parking lots, athletic fields, outdoor classrooms and playgrounds should be prioritized.

Building Phones

Emergencies can occur in the classroom at any time ranging from medical emergencies to teachers and students observing activities that they need to report. Each classroom must have the ability to call for immediate assistance. Although cellular phones may provide this ability, they cannot always be a reliable source.

Schools are constructed with concrete and steel which can both interfere with cell phone reception. Depending on where an emergency may occur within the building there may not be cellular service in that area. It is therefore essential that all classrooms be equipped with a landline telephone that allows teachers the ability to call 911.

Newer building phone systems offer intercom features that allow schools to relay messages simultaneously to everyone in the building the same as a public address system. Many older schools are replacing their original PA systems that were installed when the school was built with these types of phone systems that provide classrooms and offices with the ability to have an outside line as well as an intercom to send and receive messages within the school.

When considering this option, I caution schools to not overlook the importance of external communication and encourage them to include the integration of an outdoor speaker system that allows the intercom message to also be broadcasted in all outdoor areas mentioned above.

Two Way Radio's

A two-way radio network allows users to send a message that is received by all other radio users simultaneously, allowing for an immediate campus-wide response. This provides users with "one-to-many" communication ability. Since crisis situations are very fluid, updated information can be disseminated to all who need it in a timely manner. Without an effective means of crisis communication, the proper response as well as command and control do not exist.

To establish a solid crisis communication network, ensure that all facilities personnel, security personnel, athletics staff, receptionist, nurses and administrators are outfitted with a reliable two-way radio that is powerful enough to transmit from anywhere on your campus to include all areas of every building as well as ideally your off-campus evacuation site and your rally points. The benefit to this type of communication is paramount in an emergency when clear communication is most critical.

Outdoor environments are separate spaces from the internal walls of a school and can create vulnerabilities and communication challenges for those who are supervising students in these areas.

I strongly recommend that anyone who has students outdoors at any time of the day for any type of activity to include outdoor learning, recess, gym class, sports etc. have a two-way radio with them. This will allow them to quickly notify others on campus if they need assistance for any type of emergency that they may encounter.

Effective communication that is utilized in daily practice by your staff members will establish the groundwork for their readiness to communicate during a crisis.

Cell Phones (Text Messages, Emails and Safety Apps)

Cell phones have become incredible tools in our society, but while cell phone alert technology has become popular in recent years, it's only completely effective with an integrated mass communication system. The bottom line is, the faculty, staff and students who don't have their phones turned on, their phones are in silent or vibrate mode or for those who keep their phones deep inside their backpacks, and purses will likely never receive warnings. So again, can cell phones be useful? The answer is yes, but don't rely on them as your only means of mass communication.

Text Messages
Text messaging offers a quick and reliable way for schools to communicate with students, parents, and staff, especially for urgent or important updates like school closures, early dismissals, and emergency alerts. People are more likely to read and respond to text messages than emails or other forms of communication.

Communications

Emails

Email notification is a slower, more basic means of communication but serves its purpose in the grand scheme of things when it comes to redundancy. Covering all your bases isn't a bad idea when it comes to Mass Communications. Utilizing just email for notification purposes is not recommended but adding it to the list of other more instant means of notification doesn't hurt.

Safety and Security Apps

There are many different types of safety apps on the market today which can be confusing when trying to determine which one works the best. With most current apps when an authorized user activates the emergency function, 911 and key school employees are quickly notified so that first responders and users who have deployed the app are simultaneously informed about the emergency type and incident location.

There can also be some drawbacks such as a safety app has to be compatible with all your employees' phones to be 100% useable. For example, many apps are not compatible with Android. Non cellular service areas in your buildings and on your campus can be an issue.

School safety apps are sometimes hard to use or require a lot of navigation to use them. All apps also must receive regular updates. You'll also have to devote time to teaching people about new features, updates, and differences in the app operating systems.

If you are considering adding an app to your mass communications suite, make sure to do your homework first and vet the companies you are considering. The app should be easy to learn as well as easy for your employees to use. Ask for a trial run and pay attention to how the app can be integrated into your current operating platform as well as how it handles multiple pieces of technology and observe if it's being updated consistently.

Digital Signboards

Digital signs have been popular in recent years because of their abundance of applications. They are used by businesses to promote their products and services. They are also used in restaurants to display their menu or in stores to inform buyers of what they are selling. In-store entertainment has also been possible because of digital signage. Another popular application, although often overlooked by many, would be in the form of emergency digital signage. Digital signs can also be used for emergency communication and crisis management.

There are many ways by which an organization can make use of emergency digital signage, such as the following:

- Evacuation routes in case of emergencies like fire.
- Safety steps that should be taken during a crisis.
- Ask people to clear the route to give way to emergency responders.
- Ask people to stay calm amidst the ongoing situation.
- Inform others about upcoming weather disturbances.
- Direct traffic to a different route.
- Constantly remind people to stay safe.

Among others, one of its benefits would be related to its visibility. They can be easily seen by people and increase the likelihood that digital information can be disseminated in the most effective manner that is possible.

Another good thing about emergency digital signage is that it can warn even the people who are hearing-impaired or even the visual impaired (when you also add an audio warning). They can be easily notified in case of emergency situations, and like others, they will be able to demonstrate a high level of preparedness. The sign is highly visible, making it perfect to inform people even at night. You can be assured that everyone will see it, especially if it is big enough to be easily noticed.

Customization is another reason why emergency digital signage can prove to be a good investment. Users of this can customize messages, and they can also create a default message, which can be shown even without an internet connection. It can be modified in different languages and can be designed in such a way as the client desires. Owners can work with the providers in order to have the messages tailor-fitted based on their specifications.

Lastly, and perhaps most importantly, emergency digital signage has a sense of urgency, which is perhaps the most important in emergency situations. Messages can be displayed immediately based on what is needed in a particular instance. It can be controlled from a remote location, and it can provide real-time information, increasing the likelihood of demonstrating a more effective emergency response.

Panic Buttons

Panic buttons can provide immediate police dispatch during an emergency. These devices garner quick and targeted police responses to help control a situation immediately. In addition to administrative offices, it is recommended that each reception area is equipped with panic buttons. Panic buttons can be installed in strategic locations and can also be wireless and wearable so they can be carried with key personnel.

Integration with Existing Systems

A mass notification system should not operate in isolation but should instead be integrated with your school's existing infrastructure for seamless communication and response. Review your school's current technology setup and prioritize integration with systems such as alarms, video surveillance, and student information systems.

With such a variety of alert technologies available it is recommended that a school uses more than one method to ensure individuals are effectively and sufficiently warned about an impending threat. These technologies blanket an area and can be used to alert students, staff and faculty who are inside multiple campus buildings, as well as outdoor spaces like parking lots, green spaces and more.

Furthermore, as mentioned above these advanced technologies can be used to alert individuals about a variety of threats, including weather-related events like tornadoes and floods, as well as man-made events, like active shooters and more.

When integrated, these technologies create an effective emergency management platform that allows campuses to quickly and easily alert individuals of any impending threat, keeping students, staff and faculty out of harm's way.

Once an integrated mass communication system is in place (and rigorously tested), emergency managers and campus officials must work to inform students, staff and faculty about the system to ensure buy-in and awareness of the alerts. A system is only effective if individuals understand the threats and the directions provided, which means marketing and building awareness of the system is critical for success.

No one technology should be relied upon independently from an entire integrated system. The short-sighted approach of using only one technology puts individuals in danger and creates risks that can be easily overcome with a fully integrated system.

Assessing Your Needs and Choosing the Right System

Before selecting a mass notification and mass communication system, I recommend conducting a thorough needs assessment to tailor the system to your school's specific requirements. Consideration should be made using the following tips.

1. List all the mass notification types your school is likely to need and prioritize emergencies that require the most robust response. Be sure not to forget to include routine notifications.
2. Consider all message channels and formats and ensure the system supports multiple channels like text, email, and social media to make it accessible to a wide range of your school community.
3. Compare your budget versus the cost of poor mitigation and response. Understand that a cost-effective solution is important but investing in a comprehensive system is often far less expensive than the repercussions from a crisis that was mismanaged due to poor communication.

Be sure to select a mass notification system and mass communication system that aligns with your school's needs and budget. Consider the essential features below when making your decision.

1. Data Security and Privacy: Ensure that the system complies with privacy regulations to protect sensitive student and staff information with strong encryption and secure access protocols.
2. System Administration: Choose a system that allows your IT staff to easily configure and manage it with tools to automate tasks and streamline updates.
3. User-Friendliness: Choose a system that has an intuitive interface to allow your staff to quickly and efficiently send alerts during emergencies. Having a user-friendly design will reduce errors and training time.

Training and Testing the System

Training your staff and students with easy-to-follow guidelines on how to use the mass notification system and mass communication system is crucial to its effectiveness, especially during emergencies. Be sure to choose a provider that offers ongoing support services that include training, updates, and troubleshooting assistance, so the system remains fully operational and easy to use over time.

Conducting regular system tests and drills are also crucial for ensuring your mass notification system functions properly during emergencies. Conducting exercises will help staff and students get familiar with it. It also allows you to find and fix any issues in the system.

When conducting drills consider using the following tips.

1. Announce the drill. Begin the test alert with "THIS IS A DRILL" to prevent causing panic, especially in young students.
2. Test all channels. Verify that all communication channels are functioning properly so that no one is left out of the communication loop.
3. Notify law enforcement and first responders. Inform your local authorities so that they are aware of the exercise and know that it is just a drill and not a real event. This will also allow them to provide support if needed.

Use Clear and Easy to Follow Communication Protocols

Using pre-scripted messages and communication protocols will ensure consistency. Messages should be clear and concise which will prevent confusion and make it easy for recipients to respond quickly. For example, a standard pre-scripted emergency alert message for severe weather might read: "Severe weather warning in effect until 3:00 PM. Take shelter in designated safe areas immediately. Stay indoors until further notice." A straightforward message like this helps eliminate confusion and will ensure that everyone understands what they are supposed to do.

Encourage User Feedback

Allowing users to provide feedback will improve the effectiveness of your mass notification system and mass communication system. Feedback will help to identify potential issues and areas for improvement which will make the system more reliable and user-friendly.

Consult your technology provider to ensure they will offer support with collecting and analyzing feedback. This will ensure that your school and its mass notification system and mass communication system will continue to make the improvements and adaptations that are needed.

Summary

Schools that utilize mass notification and communication systems can significantly improve their response. With the right system and provider, they can empower their community to stay informed, be confident, organized, and ultimately be ready to respond. These systems should be tested regularly to ensure they are in working order.

Having comprehensive emergency policies and procedures is vital for schools to ensure the safety and well-being of students and staff during emergencies. Emergency policies and procedures provide a framework for quick, effective, and coordinated responses to various crises, and can reduce the impact of an incident that does occur.

Emergency planning can also help schools identify and address gaps in procedures and empower school staff and local first responders to understand and manage their responsibilities, minimizing potential harm and facilitating a more rapid return to normal operations.

Terminology

Some schools are still using terminology such as "Code Red" or "Code Blue" and other colors as emergency protocols to identify different types of emergencies. The National Standard of Best Practice with language and color codes is to move away from all code words and use of colors (i.e. "Code Red", "Code Blue") and move to plain language that's easily understood with a basic functional threat response. Basically, this means it's better to use plain simple and easy to understand English when making an emergency announcement.

Quick Reference Emergency Procedure Guide

The development of a single page, two-sided reference guide that is quickly and easily followed by everyone during an emergency is essential to supporting an effective response. This guide must include all the emergency response procedures for Lockdown, Evacuate and Shelter (L.E.S.) as well as medical emergencies, missing people, bomb threats, and should also include emergency contact names and numbers.

Employees and Guests with or without Emergency Preparedness training can easily follow the instructions given on the guide and therefore can safely respond to an emergency consistent with your response procedures. It is recommended that these wall guides be hung on the wall inside of every room of every building throughout your campus so anyone and everyone can reference the guide during an emergency and take it with them during an evacuation, if need be.

Emergency Operations Plan (EOP)

The purpose of an Emergency Operations Plan (EOP) or often referred to in the school world as School Emergency Operations Plan (SEOP) is to allow your administrative staff the ability to identify and respond to incidents by outlining the responsibilities and duties of the school and its employees.

A comprehensive plan mitigates and controls risk to the school, including life, physical assets and school brand. Developing, maintaining, and exercising the plan empowers employees during an incident to act quickly and knowledgably. In addition, the plan educates staff, faculty, students, and other key stakeholders on their roles and responsibilities before, during, and after an incident.

Having a complete plan also provides parents and other members of the community with assurances that the school has established guidelines and procedures to respond to incidents/hazards in an effective way.

In many cases, school administrators are given solutions to problems they didn't even realize existed. Very often this leads to a significant investment in security technology that looks impressive on the surface but results in no real improvement in the security posture of the institution. The best way for an educational institution to begin to create a firm foundation for the safety and security of its faculty, staff, students, and visitors is by drafting a clear plan.

A well thought out Emergency Operations Plan, developed through a collaborative process involving constituents throughout the school and surrounding community, is the basis for any incident response. For the plan to function as intended, it must be site-specific and set clear goals. A school employee should be able to articulate why they take a specific action, and why that action is a priority over something else.

There is no one-size-fits-all model for an Emergency Operations Plan. Each school has a unique community, environment, and culture with unique needs. Therefore, the Emergency Operations Plan, to be truly effective, must be tailored to the school's specific needs. Because the day-to-day realities at a school are constantly changing, the plan must be considered a work in progress.

For example, lessons learned from past or on-going incidents should be noted and taken into consideration for suggested revisions to the exisiting plan to provide for future best practices. In addition, After Action Reports (AAR) should be completed after each drill, exercise and real-life incident. Administrative teams should review each AAR in a timely manner and the information gathered in the AAR should be considered as the Emergency Operations Plan is updated.

All Emergency Operations Plans should comply with state and local laws and adhere to the standards set forth in Presidential Policy Directive 8, National Preparedness. PPD-8 calls for a coordinated and unified system with a common terminology and approach. Plans should be constructed around an "all-hazards" approach to preparedness. EOP's should also include functional or incident annexes to describe any unique requirements for particular threats or scenarios, as needed.

PPD-8 can be viewed in the context of the following five mission areas applied to school crisis incident management:

1. Prevention of potential or actual school emergencies.
2. Protection of faculty, staff, students, visitors, and the physical school property, as well as its brand image.
3. Mitigation of potential or actual harm to the school by either reducing the likelihood of an incident occurring or lessening its impact.
4. Response that utilizes Incident Command System (ICS) principles to stabilize an emergency and once again establish a safe and secure school environment and facilitates the transition to the recovery phase.
5. Recovery, or returning to the school's core mission providing a quality education.

The plan should also include procedures for the disabled and special needs population. Include provisions to assist students, staff, or visitors who use wheelchairs or other mobility devices, are deaf, blind, or have emotional needs as well as other needs requiring accommodation.

Incident Command System (ICS)

The Incident Command System (ICS) was developed to identify the primary activities and functions necessary to effectively respond to incidents. Incidents can vary in size, severity and complexity. Having a properly organized and trained personnel structure that is prepared to respond to an incident can mitigate its impact.

FEMA provides an Incident Command System structure that is globally recognized and followed by all responding agencies and their personnel. The Incident Command System (ICS) is a management system designed to enable effective and efficient domestic incident management by integrating a combination of facilities, equipment, personnel, procedures, and communications operating within a common organizational structure.

ICS provides a standardized approach using common language and framework for all responders, regardless of their agency or role, facilitating smooth collaboration and coordination. The ICS organizational structure is designed to be adaptable, allowing schools to respond effectively to a wide range of potential emergencies, from natural disasters to active shooter situations. It is also flexible and can be scaled up or down based on the size and complexity of the incident.

School Incident Command Teams (ICT) should be tailored to fit the manpower and resources that a particular school has available. Schools that have an Incident Command Teams in place will be prepared to support and work in unison with all responders that arrive on their campus for an emergency.

ICS is crucial for schools because it provides a structured, organized approach to managing emergencies, ensuring efficient response, clear communication, and effective resource allocation, ultimately prioritizing the safety of students and staff.

ICS establishes a clear chain of command and hierarchy with defined roles and responsibilities, ensuring that everyone understands their duties and who to report to during an incident. Each school ICT position and the duties assigned have been developed to work with corresponding emergency responder ICT positions in what's referred to as Unified Command.

In a school setting, a Unified Command within the Incident Command System means multiple agencies, like local police, fire, and the school itself, work together to manage an emergency. This shared decision-making approach, rather than having one single Incident Commander, is particularly useful in complex or large-scale incidents.

Some key aspects and benefits of a Unified Command during a school crisis would include shared leadership, meaning that multiple Incident Commanders, each representing their respective agency, collaboratively lead the response.

Having a Unified Incident Action Plan is another benefit because when a single plan is developed it will outline shared goals and strategies for responding to the incident. The Unified Command also coordinates and facilitates the sharing and allocation of resources among agencies, ensuring efficient use of personnel, equipment, and supplies.

Having established an Incident Command Post (ICP) as a single designated location that serves as the central hub for collaboration and decision-making will optimize the use of resources, ensuring that the right personnel and equipment are deployed at the right time and place.

The Incident Command Post is where Incident Commanders and their teams manage and deploy resources (personnel, equipment, supplies) to effectively address the incident. It also provides a centralized point for tracking and documenting all actions taken during the incident, ensuring accountability and a comprehensive record of the event.

ICS requires training and practice to ensure that school staff members are familiar with their roles and responsibilities in their ICT so that the system and team can be implemented effectively in real time.

Option Based Response for Active Shooter / Active Attacker Incidents

In an active shooter or active attacker situation at school, an option-based response allows individuals to assess the situation and choose the most effective action to increase their chances of survival.

This contrasts with traditional lockdowns, which are limited in scope. Traditional lockdown procedures focus on staying in place, hiding, and waiting for law enforcement, which can be limited in effectiveness, especially if the shooter is actively moving.

An option-based response empowers individuals to make decisions based on the specific situation, such as evacuating, barricading themselves in a room, or taking action against the shooter.

The original option-based response to an active shooter scenario is the "Run, Hide, Fight" method which was initially conceived and developed by the City of Houston, Texas in 2012 with funding from the Department of Homeland Security (DHS). The goal was to create a simple, easy-to-remember message that the public could use to respond to an active shooter situation.

The phrase "Run Hide Fight" originated as part of a training video and was designed to provide a clear and memorable set of instructions for individuals to follow. The Run, Hide, Fight method is a simple, three-step approach to help individuals respond during such emergencies.

The U.S. Department of Homeland Security (DHS), the FBI and many law enforcement agencies worldwide endorse "Run, Hide, Fight" as a simple yet effective strategy for surviving an active shooter, and it's often used in schools and other settings. If you haven't adopted an option-based response protocol, I encourage you to do so.

It's important to mention that since the inception of "Run Hide Fight" there have been many companies with offshoot models that have surfaced and created confusion for those who are looking to adopt an option-based response model in their school.

These companies, and their models, have simply word smithed

the original "Run Hide Fight" protocols for example, changing the word "run" to avoid or evacuate and changing the word "fight" to defend or counter. Many of these offshoot models have not only overcomplicated the basics of "Run Hide Fight" they have also been confusing, difficult to understand, and challenging to remember for the average person.

Regardless of what option-based response method your school chooses to use, the most important aspect is training and training frequency. Implementing and maintaining an option-based response protocol at your school requires comprehensive training for all personnel, including teachers, staff, and students, to understand the different response options and how to apply them effectively.

Ideally conducting this training at least once per year will keep the protocols fresh in everyone's mind. Annual training will also help your staff develop and maintain the confidence and decision-making skills necessary to keep themselves and their students safe.

There are many active shooter response training programs and instructors to choose from so it's best to do your due diligence before choosing one. Before choosing a company and instructor you should check references from other schools that have used the company and instructor to confirm that they have been well received without issues. You should also check the instructor's training background to confirm that they are qualified.

Choosing the right company and instructor who utilizes a training model that includes an in-person presentation, detailed demonstrations and practical exercises (scenarios) is vital to not only how well the content will be received by your staff but also how much of what they are taught will be retained by them.

How this content is delivered is extremely important therefore you should request to see their training curriculum and ensure that they have a training method that is thorough, non-traumatic and executed in a controlled environment. Many companies take a law enforcement approach to their training method. This approach is often a hardened, more callus delivery that is suited for law enforcement personnel and not educators.

Ensure that they are not utilizing a violent approach. For example, the use of training weapons that fire projectiles at participants, conduct scenarios that are too fast paced that result in people running, instructors that chase and or contact participants, and the use of fake blood to simulate wounded people.

You should also confirm that the curriculum has safety protocols in place for scenario training to include a set of rules and parameters that are given to participants, the use of two way radios that allows participants to communicate with the instructor at all times, and an option that allows individuals who have concerns such as medical conditions, anxiety disorders and PTSD to opt out of participation prior to scenarios.

Making the transition from a traditional lockdown method to an option-based response model can be a big step for schools. This transition is often met with concerns from both staff members and parents, which is why I suggest taking what I refer to as a crawl, walk, run approach. This approach should include a transition plan and correspondence.

Choose a company that can support your transition process who has the ability to provide you with documents such as staff and parent letters that address common concerns with Q and A's and prior school client endorsements, a training day overview that you can send to staff members in advance of training day that allows them to understand the itinerary and know what to expect.

In addition, using a company that can provide you with a comprehensive lockdown drill guide that you can use once the staff training is complete is also important. This guide should include topics such as age-appropriate response levels, future lockdown drill scripts, drill checklist, teacher talking points that are age appropriate for their grade level and after-action report templates.

Threat Assessment Team Model

A school threat assessment team is a multidisciplinary group tasked with identifying, evaluating, and managing potential threats to school safety. This team typically includes school administrators, mental health professionals, teachers, and law enforcement personnel. The goal is to prevent violence by intervening early and providing support before a situation escalates.

The following recommendations have been provided by the United States Secret Service National Threat Assessment Center (NTAC). The NTAC report titled Enhancing School Safety Using Threat Assessment Model: An Operational Guide for Preventing Targeted School Violence provides best practices for schools to help develop comprehensive behavioral threat assessments and targeted violence prevention plans.

Recommendations include:

- Establish a multidisciplinary threat assessment team.
  - This should be a team of school personnel including faculty, staff, administrators, coaches, and available school personnel who will direct, manage, and document the threat assessment process.
- Define behaviors that would trigger immediate intervention.
  - (e.g., threats, violent acts, weapons on campus)
- Establish and provide training on a central reporting system.
  - This can include an online form on the school website, email address, phone number, or smartphone application. Ensure that it provides anonymity to those reporting concerns.
- Determine the threshold for law enforcement intervention.
- Establish threat assessment procedures.
  - This should include practices for maintaining documentation, identifying sources of information, reviewing records, and conducting interviews.
- Develop risk management options.
  - Create individualized management plans to mitigate identified risks, notify law enforcement and ensure the schools safety.
- Create and promote a safe school climate.
  - The school should be built on a culture of safety, respect, trust, and emotional support. Encourage communication, intervene in conflicts and bullying, and empower students to share their concerns
- Provide training for all stakeholders.

○ This should include personnel, students, parents, and law enforcement.

The purpose behind having an established threat assessment team is to have the ability to provide early intervention by aiming to identify students, staff, or others who may pose a threat to themselves or others and intervene before a violent act occurs.

If a threat is made by an individual or an individual has been identified as exhibiting concerning behavior, the team will conduct a risk assessment to evaluate the severity of a threat, considering factors like the individual's history, mental health, and access to weapons.

After the assessment is complete, they develop and implement mitigation strategies to reduce or eliminate the risk, which may include counseling, academic interventions, or alternative placement.

Having a threat assessment team at your school is important for the following reasons:

- Prevention of Harm - Teams identify and address concerning behaviors that could lead to violence, intervening early to prevent escalation.
- Early Intervention - They recognize warning signs and provide support to students who may be struggling with mental health challenges or other issues that could contribute to risky behavior.
- Support for Students - Threat assessments help ensure that students who need mental health support receive the care they need to thrive.

- Positive School Climate - By demonstrating a commitment to safety, schools can foster a more positive and inclusive environment where students feel safe and supported.

A typical threat assessment model and process would ideally look like this:

1. Reporting - Any staff member, student, or parent can report concerning behavior or threats to a central point.
2. Initial Assessment - The team reviews the report and conducts an initial assessment to determine the nature and severity of the threat and determines if law enforcement needs to be involved.
3. Investigation - The team may conduct interviews, review records, and gather additional information to gain a better understanding of the situation.
4. Risk Assessment - The team evaluates the potential for violence, considering the individual's history, mental health, and access to weapons.
5. Mitigation Plan - Based on the risk assessment, the team develops a plan to address the threat, which may include counseling, academic interventions, or alternative placement.
6. Monitoring - The team continues to monitor the situation and adjust the plan as needed.

School threat assessment teams are crucial for proactively preventing violence and ensuring a safe learning environment by identifying and addressing potential risks before they escalate. Many States are now mandating the creation of behavioral assessment teams in public schools, focusing on identifying and addressing threats to safety.

If you haven't already, I encourage you to establish and develop a multi-disciplinary threat assessment model for your school with a team that has been trained in the current standards of threat assessment and has the tools necessary to conduct and support the threat assessment process.

Student Parent Reunification Plan

A Student Parent Reunification is the means for the safe and orderly reunion of students and families when it is necessary to release students directly to their parent, guardian or designated emergency contact in the event of an emergency evacuation or school closing has occurred that prevents a normal dismissal.

There are a variety of emergency situations which may require the activation of a Student Parent Reunification that include, but are not limited to, Fire or Damage to a School Building, Natural Disaster, Field Trip Emergency or School Bus Accident, Violence in the Surrounding Community, and a Situation involving a Threat, Weapons or Violence at School.

Under any circumstance, the process may prove challenging, and emotions will run high. Because of this, the need to develop a plan and provide a coordinated response prior to the chaos of an emergency is essential.

In planning for Student Parent Reunification, the characteristics of the hazard and its magnitude, intensity, speed of onset, and anticipated duration are all significant factors. These will determine the number of staff needed, the number of people to be reunited, the need for reception facilities, the extent of traffic control and security required.

Your district and/or school(s) must be prepared to conduct both small-scale and large-scale reunification at all times of the day both from known hazard areas and from unexpected incident locations.

A well-organized Student Parent Reunification process will help to reduce anxiety during a potentially stressful situation and reunite children with their families in a structured, timely and safe manner.

Having a defined process with an established visibly planned structure reflects a sense of organization and professionalism in an emergency. This, in turn, may provide calm and order in what surely will be an extraordinarily stressful event. In addition to providing coordination between reunification partners, the plan also assures that children are returned to the proper parent or legal guardian. No child should be released to an individual unknown to them, or who may cause them additional harm.

Once again, I'll say if your school hasn't already developed a Student Parent Reunification Plan to include identifying and training staff members who will be a part of the reunification team, I encourage you to do so.

Having multiple evacuation and operational sites that all serve a specific purpose is a critical component of a school's emergency preparedness plan. Establishing these sites as discussed below will allow for effective emergency response, and minimize harm to students, staff, and the community.

On Campus Evacuation Site

I would assume that most, if not all of you, who are reading this book have an established on-campus evacuation site. This is a location on your campus in close proximity to your school where you go when you conduct an organized evacuation for emergencies such as a building fire.

This location should be a minimum of three hundred feet from the closest building by fire code. In certain cases, some schools that have multiple buildings that house different grade levels have on campus evacuation sites for each. An example would be that a K-12 school that has a separate building for its kindergarten through fifth grade (elementary or lower school), sixth grade through eighth grade (middle school) and ninth through twelfth grade (high or upper school) may have separate on campus evacuation sites for each building.

When choosing or reassessing your on-campus evacuation site it's important to keep several factors in mind. The first would be to choose a location that is large enough to accommodate your entire population of students, staff members and potentially visitors. The second would be to choose a location that is accessible for the disabled and special needs population, and the third would be to choose a location that is out of the way of emergency responders and the different types of emergency vehicles that may be entering your campus.

Off Campus Evacuation Site

Having a location that is not on your campus where you can move everyone in an organized manner is necessary when your on-campus evacuation site is too close for the emergency situation. Ideally this site should be within walking distance and should be large enough to accommodate the number of staff and students that you have.

An example would be if you evacuated everyone to your on-campus evacuation site for a fire and the prevailing wind was blowing smoke and embers into the area where everyone was. In this case you will obviously need to move everyone to a safer location that is farther away and out of the prevailing wind.

Another example would be if there was an outdoor gas leak on your campus and your on-campus evacuation site was again too close to the danger zone and or the fire department ordered you to move everyone farther away if not off of the campus to allow responders to contain and control the leak you would need a predetermined off-campus location where you could move everyone to.

A third example would be if you had a bomb threat and based on the information provided in the threat responders ordered you to move everyone to a safe distance which would require you to relocate off the campus.

Hopefully I have made my point in that having a predetermined off-campus evacuation site is a standard best practice and if you haven't established one, I would encourage you to do so.

It's important to keep in mind that if you must move everyone off campus there is the likelihood that you may not be able to return during that school day which means that in many cases off-campus evacuations will result in student parent reunification which we will discuss in detail a couple of paragraphs from now.

I mention this because having an off-campus evacuation site that has the ability to also serve as a Student Parent Reunification Site is ideal. This will prevent you from having to relocate everyone to another location for reunification.

You should also consider that if any of this occurs during inclement weather or extreme hot or cold conditions it will be challenging at best to expect people to remain outdoors for an extended period of time. For this reason, many schools try to facilitate an off-campus evacuation site that has indoor accommodation such as another school in the area or a local house of worship (church, synagogue, temple, etc.).

It is also a good idea to establish a Memorandum of Understanding (MOU) and Memorandum of Agreement (MOA) with the owners or managers of the site. An MOU is meant to assist and define the relationship between agencies or organizations in emergencies. Be sure to have a signed MOU and MOA with the property owner in place before you choose a site rather than assume it's okay to use for this purpose.

Off Campus Rally Points

Rally points are crucial for school safety, serving as designated meeting places during emergencies like Active Shooter / Active Attacker incidents. They allow for quick and organized reunification of students and staff, facilitating accountability and ensuring everyone has evacuated to a safe location.

If your school has established an option-based response protocol "Run Hide Fight" for Active Shooter / Active Attacker incidents there will be individuals who are self-evacuating if an incident occurs. Having at least two Off Campus "Rally Points" located in opposite directions of your campus will provide individuals a choice and give them the ability to move in multiple directions.

In situations like this it's important that those who have been able to evacuate the building have the ability to distance themselves by moving away from the threat and not have to exit the building and move back through or past the danger zone where the threat is located. Having multiple Rally Points (two or more) in different directions will provide directional options for those who have gotten out.

Designated rally points are a key component of school emergency plans, and quick reference emergency guide maps indicating their locations in addition to regular drills help students and staff become familiar with the "Run" (self-evacuation) portion of "Run Hide Fight" and the location of the rally points for when they're evacuating in this manner.

Student Parent Reunification Site

In cases where it is not safe to remain on campus, return to campus after an off-campus evacuation, or where parents coming to and leaving the school may create more of a hazard, a Student Parent Reunification will need to take place Off-Campus at a location referred to as a Student Parent Reunification Site.

Logistically, this is much more challenging since students and staff will need to be moved, either by bus or on foot, to the reunification site. Securing and supervising students while in transit requires extra planning and diligence, and it may take time for bus drivers to report in.

The decision to implement an Off-Campus Reunification will need to be made early in the crisis, if possible, BEFORE parents begin arriving at school. Be sure to send a mass notification to families to arrange for pick up at the Reunification site.

Off-Campus Reunification sites are divided into two categories:

1. Near Campus: sites within walking distance (ideally the best option).
2. Away from Campus: sites which require buses to transport students (logistically challenging and time-consuming).

The process of selecting a site should be done well in advance of an emergency to allow representatives from the site to participate in planning, training, and exercises. Again, as previously mentioned, it may be necessary to establish a Memorandum of

Understanding (MOU) and a Memorandum of Agreement (MOA) with the owners or managers of the site.

In some instances, the county emergency management agency may select multiple sites in the county to be used by multiple schools or districts. In this instance, the emergency management agency would determine which location will be used in an emergency. Possible sites might include another school, church, other house of worship or community center.

At a minimum the following must be taken into consideration when selecting these sites:

1. Adequate road capacity leading to the site as well as accessible ingress and egress.
2. Adequate parent parking for the anticipated number of parent vehicles that will be arriving.
3. The site should be large enough to accommodate the number of students and parents that will be arriving.
4. The site should be accessible by those with special accessibility and functional needs.
5. There should be a means to place students away (out-of-sight if possible) from the parent waiting area to ensure order and accountability is maintained.
6. The building / site should contain separate rooms / areas for providing mental health services, notifications, law enforcement activities, and first aid.
7. Adequate staffing to initially set the site up, direct parents as they arrive, answer questions, assist parents with filling out reunification cards, check parent identification, retrieve students as their parents arrive, reunite students with their caregivers and maintain calm and order throughout reunification efforts.

8. Organizers should provide adequate distance between the media and the reunification site. Identify a designated location in advance for the media to gather. This location should be off site (a separate location) and should limit their ability to capture images and video to maintain student and parent privacy.

Incident Command Post

In the context of a school emergency, the Incident Command Post (ICP) is the designated location where the Incident Commander oversees all incident operations, ensuring a coordinated and efficient response.

The ICP is the central hub for managing an incident, providing a focal point for decision-making, communication, and resource allocation. The ICP can be located in a trailer, tent, or within a building, depending on the nature and scale of the incident.

It is recommended that all schools have designated Incident Command Posts and are capable of being able to operate from both an on campus ICP as well as an off-campus ICP if the on-campus location is compromised and unsafe. Typically, your school should have the ability to access the following remotely:

- Security Cameras
- Building Floor Plans
- Student Information System
- Mass Communication Systems:
- Text/email and phone alerts
  - Students
  - Faculty/Staff

- o Parents
- Speaker system
- Staff/Faculty Information System
- School Emergency Operations Plan

Campus Maps and Building Floorplans

Campus Maps are generally used for wayfinding, but oftentimes they are overlooked as an important part of security and emergency planning. These maps are multi-purpose and can be utilized in a variety of ways.

Campus maps typically show a collection of buildings, roads, parking lots, and other information relevant to finding your way around and they are also beneficial for security and emergency response purposes.

The main purpose of Campus Maps is to provide some form of direction. These maps are generally used by visitors but can also be used by employees and students who need to know how to get from one place to another. They are essential tools for making campuses navigationally friendly. Even those who have worked on a campus for several years may need to access a previously unknown area, rendering such information beneficial to all.

Building Floorplans, on the other hand, are generally used by contractors to reference specific locations within the building to help them navigate and make repairs and modifications but they can also be beneficial for security and emergency response purposes. They often serve as a tool to identify the layout of walls and doors both internally and externally as well as all utilities that are housed within the building.

Evacuation Sites and Operational Locations

While you may initially think of a campus map as only a directional tool and a building floorplan as a reference tool there are plenty of instances where they are used for Security. Hospitals, Offices, Manufacturing Facilities, and Schools use Campus Maps and Building Floorplans to plan for a wide range of emergencies.

Campus Maps and Building Floorplans when keyed with the locations of emergency specific hardware such as Fire Hydrant Locations, Security Camera Locations, Exterior Door and Window Numbering, and Utility Shutoff Locations can prove useful to emergency responders when they arrive to mitigate a situation.

One of the most crucial times to have access to a Campus Security Map or Building Floorplan is when you have very little time at all. Emergencies often arise without warning and losing seconds or even minutes can cost the safety and lives of those on your campus. Developing these maps and plans in advance of a crisis can prove invaluable.

Having trained personnel to act as a deterrence is a significant component of a comprehensive school security program to promote a safe and secure environment conducive to learning. However, it is essential to consider both the benefits and potential drawbacks of in-house security verses contract security and implement these measures in a way that fosters a safe, supportive, and positive environment for all members of the school community.

Security Guards

Campus security guards offer several benefits, including a safer learning environment, reduced bullying and crime, and enhanced emergency response.

The presence of security guard's acts as a visible deterrent to potential threats, discouraging individuals with malicious intent from entering the school. Security guards can manage who enters and exits the school, ensuring only authorized individuals are on campus. They monitor the school premises both on foot as well as with surveillance cameras, looking for suspicious activity and potential threats.

Security guards can act as a liaison with law enforcement, and they are trained to respond to emergencies, providing immediate assistance and coordinating with emergency services. They can also build positive relationships with staff members and students, which helps to prevent and address safety issues.

The presence of security guards can reduce instances of bullying, fights, and other disciplinary issues. Security guards can build trust and rapport with students, encouraging them to report safety concerns and potential threats. By addressing issues proactively, they can also help reduce suspensions and other disciplinary actions.

In addition, the presence of security guards can create a sense of calm and safety, allowing students to focus on learning without worrying about safety concerns and can relieve some of the burden on teachers and staff, allowing them to focus on teaching and administration. Knowing that security guards are on campus can also provide parents with peace of mind about their children's safety.

When it comes to security guards, schools have two options. The first would be to hire a contract security guard company and the second would be to hire individuals themselves, which is commonly known as "in house" security. There can be advantages as well as disadvantages to each choice. For school security, the decision between in-house guards and a contracted security company involves balancing control, cost, and flexibility.

Contracted security companies offer flexibility, potentially lower costs, and delegated risk, but may have less control over specific guard training and company culture. Hiring a security company may reduce such things as liability, in-house training require-ments, staff management, scheduling and uniform expenses.

On the downside, unfortunately in most cases you will have limited or no input when it comes to choosing the individuals who are assigned to work at your school. This can create issues for many schools for several reasons.

Examples being, if a younger security guard who is not much older than your student population is placed on your campus, he or she may interact inappropriately with your students. An older security guard with limited mobility may not be able to perform their duties sufficiently. If this individual does not have good people skills they will not be received well by your staff, students and parents. In addition, most contract security guard company training programs are basic and consist of generalized training topics that in most cases do not include specific campus security training protocols in the curriculum.

On the other hand, in-house security offers more control over hiring, training, and culture alignment, but requires more administrative effort and cost. Hiring in-house will allow you to be more selective but will require you to establish a formalized security guard training program, designate someone to manage the program, establish post orders and standard operating procedures for the guards, purchase uniforms, equipment and maintain inventory.

In addition, you may also be required to hold a state security company license if required by your state as well as have the proper insurance in place to reduce liability. For comparison's sake I have broken down the pros and cons of both options:

Physical Security

Contracted Security:
    Pros:

- Lower initial costs and administrative burden for hiring and training.
- Flexibility with staffing levels and adjusting to specific needs.
- Delegated risk, with the security company handling liability.

    Cons:

- Less control over hiring, training, and performance standards.
- Potential for higher costs depending on the scope of services.
- May require more coordination and management of the contract.

In-House Security:
    Pros:

- Greater control over hiring, training, and performance standards.
- Potential for stronger loyalty and familiarity with school culture.
- Direct oversight and management of security personnel.

Cons:

- Higher administrative burden for hiring, training, and payroll.
- Potentially higher costs due to salary, benefits, uniforms, equipment and overhead.
- Less flexibility with adjusting staffing levels to changing needs.

Obviously, there are several factors to consider when choosing which option is best for your school. The first would be the size of your school and your budget. Larger schools with more resources might find in-house security more feasible, while smaller schools or those with tighter budgets may prefer contracted services.

The second would be your specific security needs. Schools with unique security requirements, such as a need for specialized training or a specific cultural alignment, might prefer in-house security.

The third would be your desire for control. Schools that prioritize control over every aspect of their security program may opt for in-house security.

The forth consideration would be your flexibility and scalability. Schools that need the ability to quickly adjust staffing levels or add security services based on events or threats might find contracted services more beneficial.

The fifth would be risk management. Schools that want to delegate some of the legal and financial risks associated with security may find contracted services attractive.

Physical Security

Ultimately, the best choice depends on the specific needs and priorities of your school. Some schools may find a hybrid approach, with some in-house staff and some contracted services, to be the most effective choice. Regardless, both options should be evaluated by your risk management and or legal team before choosing which option is best suited for your school.

Daily responsibilities of a school security guard at a minimum should include patrolling the entire campus and the interior and exterior of all buildings, responding to incidents, calling for law enforcement support if necessary and writing incident reports.

Daily duties should include checking all building doors, windows, interior and exterior lights, and fences and gates to make sure they are intact, not damaged, locked and functioning properly. School security guards may also work at the reception desk, monitor surveillance cameras, greet visitors, operate a visitor management system, direct traffic and provide crowd control during special events.

The qualifications and skills you should seek in all security guards who will work on your campus should include them having prior security experience as well as being more than just a few years older than your student population. A security guard with a more seasoned background such as those who have served in the military or are veterans of a police force may be an even better choice.

You may also require that your security guards have CPR/AED and First Aid certifications. Licensing requirements vary by state, but most states mandate that a security officer hold a current valid security guard license from the state in which they are working in before beginning work as a campus security officer.

In recent years it has become increasingly more common for schools to use armed security. I am not against this, but I do heed caution when considering. The level of training required to assume the responsibility of carrying a firearm on a school campus is extensive for many reasons.

In law enforcement the use of force is measured by what's commonly known as the "use of force continuum". This guideline helps officers determine the appropriate level of force to use in different situations, starting with minimal force (like presence or verbal commands).

The next level would escalate to more forceful methods like physical restraint, less-lethal weapons (pepper spray, taser, baton), and the highest level on the continuum would ultimately be the use of deadly force (firearm).

For armed school security this means if they have not been trained in the use of force and do not have all of the intermediary weapons to use between minimum force and deadly force they are often faced with challenges and decisions that result in them drawing their weapon to gain control.

Unfortunately, there have been many instances where inexperienced, under trained and under equipped individuals have made bad choices which have resulted in them discharging their firearms causing unnecessary injury or death to the subject they are trying to detain.

The current standards of best practice for law enforcement responding to an active threat / active shooter situation is for that officer to engage and mitigate the threat (attacker) as quickly as possible with tactics that are commonly known as solo engagement. Law enforcement officers across the country are highly trained on a regular basis with this response.

This specialized training prepares them for high stress, extremely volatile highly populated environments and the potential use of deadly force that may be required to mitigate the threat. Without the proper training and required training frequency it is extremely unlikely that they will respond appropriately.

The point I am making is that before you choose to use armed security, I urge you to carefully consider the risk and liability involved and ensure that the individuals who will assume these roles have received and continue to receive the appropriate training required to assume this level of responsibility.

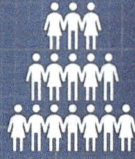

Establishing a diverse suite of specialized teams is an important component to an effective school safety and security program. Schools benefit significantly from having specialized teams, as these teams provide immediate and effective support during crises, ensuring the safety and well-being of students and staff. These teams are equipped to address both physical and emotional needs, facilitating a swift and coordinated response.

It is extremely important that each team is initially trained in their respective field as well as provided with annual or semiannual training depending on the recommended training frequency for each specific team. It is also imperative to maintain current rosters for everyone on each team to include all training dates and certification dates.

Specialized teams are trained to handle various crisis situations, allowing for a rapid and coordinated response, which can be crucial in preventing further harm and minimizing the impact of an incident. These teams include professionals like school counselors, psychologists, and social workers, who can provide immediate mental health support and crisis intervention services to students and staff.

Teams can also collaborate with local law enforcement and emergency services to ensure the safety and security of the school environment. Specialized teams act as a central point for communication and coordination during a crisis, ensuring that all parties involved are working together effectively. Certain teams and team members can also provide psychological first aid and support to those affected by a crisis, helping them cope with the emotional impact of the event and facilitate a smoother recovery process. By implementing crisis response plans and providing ongoing training, specialized teams contribute to preventing future crises and improving the overall safety and security of the school environment.

Each team listed below has its own specific purpose and role in crisis management.

Incident Command Team

Schools can benefit significantly from having an Incident Command Team (ICT), as it establishes a clear, structured, and coordinated response to emergencies, ensuring efficient resource allocation, effective communication, and ultimately, the safety of students and staff. Whether it's a man-made or natural crisis, or an act of violence in the school, a quick organized response is extremely important.

School personnel are likely to be the first on the scene when an incident occurs on school property. Eventually police, fire, emergency medical services, the utility company and others will arrive and manage the scene. However, the initial response will likely be by school employees who will begin the emergency management process until the first responders arrive and resume it with the recovery process once they leave.

Every first responder agency from across the country that responds to the schools in their area uses "Incident Command" during a crisis. The "Incident Command System" (ICS) is a response method that determines the role of everyone responding to a crisis and defines a shared vocabulary and shared expectations of behavior. Being familiar with their procedures and having the ability to work in parallel with them once they arrive with what's known as "Unified Command" is imperative to a successful outcome.

ICS is part of a National Incident Management System that integrates existing best practices into a consistent, nationwide approach to domestic incident management. The ICS is aligned with the principles of the National Incident Management System (NIMS), which promotes a common approach to emergency management across all levels of government and agencies.

The structure of ICS coordinates activities in five major functional areas: command, operations, planning, logistics, and finance administration.

ICS is flexible and scalable, allowing for functional areas to be added as necessary and discontinued when no longer necessary and facilitates coordination with external agencies, such as law enforcement and emergency medical services, ensuring a unified and effective response. The flexibility and scalability of ICS allows it to adapt to the specific needs of different emergencies, whether large or small.

The ICS also promotes the use of a common language and terminology among all responders, regardless of their agency or background, which improves communication and coordination. The ICS helps to document all aspects of the emergency response, including resource allocation, actions taken, and outcomes, which is crucial for post-incident analysis and improvement.

Specialized Teams

During a school-based critical incident, school personnel will be required to serve as first responders. In order to ensure that school personnel are prepared to potentially coordinate that response with local, state, or federal officials, an Incident Command System (ICS) component should be included in your school's Emergency Operations Plan (EOP).

Emergency responses are dynamic and require flexibility. Having the ability to make time sensitive decisions during a crisis is extremely important. The effective direction, control, and coordination of an incident requires institutional commitment and an internal understanding of roles and responsibilities. Lines of succession (backup) should be created for each of the key positions.

With that in mind, schools must understand and use the Incident Command System (ICS) as their framework for crisis management. Establishing a proper school-based Incident Command System (ICS) and an Incident Command Team (ICT) structure with members that are familiar with their positions and duties is critical when it's time to manage a crisis from onset through recovery.

An Incident Command Team (ICT) clarifies who is in charge and who reports to whom, preventing confusion and ensuring a smooth flow of information and instructions during an emergency. The ICT facilitates a structured, systematic approach to emergency planning and response, allowing for efficient resource allocation and task assignment.

The ICT also helps to ensure that resources (personnel, equipment, supplies) are used effectively and efficiently, minimizing waste and maximizing impact. The ICT will also serve as a central hub for communication, allowing for clear and timely information sharing between different teams and agencies involved in the emergency response.

By establishing a clear framework for emergency response, the Incident Command Team (ICT) can help ensure the safety of students, staff, and responders, minimizing risks and potential harm.

After the safety and status of staff and students have been assured and emergency conditions have been abated, the incident command team, teachers and school officials will be responsible for the restoration of the school's infrastructure and educational programs.

Successfully implementing an Incident Command Team (ICT) first requires structuring a team properly with the appropriate people for the appropriate positions. After the team structure is in place providing the team with adequate training in the Incident Command System (ICS) and ICT purpose and structure will be essential for their success.

In addition, providing them with dynamic training to include school crisis specific tabletop exercises will prepare them to effectively and efficiently work as a team while managing a crisis as well as understand a unified command response.

Behavioral Threat Assessment Team

A School Threat Assessment Team should be a multidisciplinary team of trained professionals that consist of school mental health professionals, administrators, safety and security directors, nurses, and athletic staff members.

Threat assessment is intended to prevent violence and involves both assessment and intervention. It involves determining whether a student or staff member poses a threat of violence, meaning they have intent and the means of carrying out the threat.

A threat assessment involves evaluation and classification of the threat (i.e., transient versus substantive) and appropriate response and intervention, including notification and involvement of parents, law enforcement and a written safety plan. Threat assessment should be a component of a comprehensive approach to maintaining a safe school, which offers a balance between physical and psychological safety.

Once a threat assessment team is established it is imperative that they receive the appropriate initial training as well as ongoing training and updates. This training focuses on behavioral threat assessment and management in a K-12 school setting and the best practices in establishing a K-12 behavioral threat assessment and management process, including the assessment of risk factors and warning signs, identification of concerns, ethical and legal considerations and follow-up interventions to include monitoring.

It is important to act quickly to any and all threats with a trained threat assessment team that has the appropriate policies and procedures to effectively handle any situation as it arises.

Student Parent Reunification Team

While school emergency situations requiring Family Reunifications are rare, they do occur with enough frequency that it is necessary to have a well-defined team and process as well as the supplies necessary to implement it. A well-organized Reunification process will help to reduce anxiety during a potentially stressful situation and reunite students with their families in a structured, timely & safe manner.

Student Parent Reunification is used when it is necessary to release students directly to their parent, guardian or designated emergency contact due to an emergency situation that prevents a normal dismissal. Situations which may require a Student Parent Reunification include but are not limited to fire, damage to a school building, natural disaster, gas leak, field trip emergency, school bus accident, violence in the surrounding community, a situation involving a threat, and weapons or violence at school etc.

It takes time, patience and diligence to implement a process like this in order to safely reunite each student with their parent, guardian or designated emergency contact.

Every emergency situation is different. Without a properly trained team with the necessary resources and materials in place this can and will be a cumbersome process that when not properly executed can expose your school to unnecessary risk and liability with regards to student care and custody.

Medical Response Team

A medical response team comprised of individuals who have been trained in Basic First Aid, Stop the Bleed, CPR and AED use who are ready to respond to a medical emergency can provide life-saving resources to victims while Emergency Medical Services (EMS) are on their way. Keeping an up-to-date team roster with individuals who have current training certifications and the equipment necessary to render aid can prove invaluable.

Watch Team

Studies show that in most previous attacks on schools the assailant had plotted their attack prior to execution. Many times, these plots were in some way carried out during the attack. These actions have included targeting School Resource Officers or Security Guards, compromising security measures by disabling security cameras, cutting phone lines, cutting power, setting off fire alarms, and disabling vehicles used by security. In several cases exterior doors were chained and or zip tied prior to the attack to prevent those who were inside from evacuating resulting in an increased number of wounded and casualties.

All the above methods mentioned are physical actions that may have been detected and mitigated prior to an attack being carried out if individuals had been trained to know what to look for as well as how to respond.

School maintenance, athletics, nursing, counseling, receptionist, administration and office staff are positions that allow them to be located internally and externally throughout a campus each day. These individuals can be trained and utilized to form a Watch Team which is an effective way of having an ongoing presence both inside and outside your school walls with a large number of people that can keep a proactive protective eye on your campus each day.

Training individuals to know what to look for is the first step in preventing an incident from occurring. Training them with the protocols on how to respond once they have identified or encountered something is the next step to mitigating the effects of the situation.

Training these individuals on the topics shown below can prepare them to serve as effective Watch Team Members:

- Campus Security Best Practices
- Visitor Management Enforcement
- Surveillance and Observational Tactics
- Elements of Detection and Deterrence
- Suspicious Activity and Behavior Recognizers
- De-escalation Techniques
- Confront, Contain, Control
- Calming and Diversion Techniques
- Bomb Threat and Suspicious Package Protocol
- Radio Communication Best Practices
- Crisis and Emergency Situation Assessment
- Responding to Emergencies

Seconds save lives during an attack and individuals must be prepared to respond quickly and effectively.

Having the appropriate medical equipment in place to respond to a diverse range of medical emergencies on your campus is essential. All the equipment listed below should be strategically placed throughout your campus in both fixed locations as well as mobile locations.

Fixed locations refers to the equipment being mounted to walls in strategic areas and easily accessible to anyone, and mobile locations refers to the equipment being located in areas such as golf carts for athletics, security and maintenance personnel as well as athletics, security and maintenance offices where they can be accessed and transported to the patient's location by staff members.

Automated External Defibrillators (AED)

AEDs (Automated External Defibrillators) are crucial in schools because they significantly increase the chances of survival for individuals experiencing sudden cardiac arrest (SCA), a leading cause of death in student athletes and on school campuses, by providing early defibrillation. Survival rates for SCA are highest with early defibrillation. For every minute that passes without defibrillation, the chances of survival decrease by 7-10%.

AEDs are portable, easy-to-use devices that can analyze a person's heart rhythm and deliver an electric shock (defibrillation) if necessary, helping the heart to restart. Studies show that schools with AEDs have significantly higher survival rates for SCA compared to schools without them. In schools with AEDs, survival rates can reach 70%, more than seven times the national average.

Having AEDs in schools can also help reduce potential legal liability for school districts if a SCA occurs on campus. The presence of AEDs sends a powerful message that the health and safety of everyone in the school is a top priority, creating a sense of security and reducing anxiety for students, staff, and parents.

It's crucial to train staff and potentially students on how to use AEDs and perform CPR, ensuring that they are prepared to respond effectively in an emergency. Having a well-rehearsed Cardiac Emergency Response Plan (CERP), which includes AEDs, CPR training for staff and potentially trained students, and clear protocols for responding to SCA, can further improve survival rates.

Automated External Defibrillators (AEDs) should be placed in strategic locations that are easily and quickly accessible. Each unit should be hanging on a wall inside a case that is alarmed if opened.

The school should have a written AED Policy. The purpose of this document is to provide for the ongoing care and maintenance of the school AEDs and to ensure that all the AED's have consistent care and maintenance. The outlined procedure should state that AEDs listed need to be checked on a regular basis to ensure they are charged and ready for use. One individual should be responsible for ordering replacement supplies for the AEDs.

Since an event requiring an AED could occur during the evening or weekend hours, a visitor may be more likely to alert personnel. It is recommended that personnel are trained to use the equipment and know the AED's location(s).

First Aid Go Kits

In case of an emergency evacuation, FEMA recommends that every classroom and the administrative office maintain a "go kit," a self-contained and portable stockpile of emergency supplies, often placed in a backpack and left in a readily accessible but secure location so that it is ready to "go."

The school emergency operations plan should reference the go kits and note the personnel to whom responsibility is delegated for stocking and replenishing them. The contents of the go kits should reflect the consideration of the school's circumstances and resources. Go Kit supply checklists typically include items such as:

- List of school emergency procedures
- Whistle
- First aid kit with instructions
- Classroom bags should contain clipboards with:
- List of classroom students
- List of students with special needs and description of needs (i.e. medical issues, prescription medicines), marked confidential.

Bleed Control Kits

Uncontrolled bleeding is a major cause of preventable death in trauma, with studies showing that it accounts for a significant percentage of pre-hospital deaths.

School bleed control kits, also known as Stop the Bleed kits, are crucial for saving lives by providing immediate access to essential supplies and training to control life-threatening bleeding in emergencies, particularly in situations like school shootings or accidents.

Schools are increasingly recognizing the importance of being prepared for a range of emergencies, including those involving traumatic injuries, and bleed control kits are a vital part of that preparedness.

Bleed control kits equip teachers, staff, and even students with the tools and knowledge to act quickly and effectively until professional help arrives.

Bleed control kits consist of gauze and tourniquets. In addition to packing these items in First Aid Kits, staff and faculty should be taught life-saving techniques on how to "Stop the Bleed" in an emergency (applying pressure, packing a wound, tying a tourniquet). By providing immediate access to supplies like tourniquets and pressure bandages, these kits can significantly improve the chances of survival for individuals with severe bleeding.

Alongside providing the kits, schools should also offer training to staff and students on how to use them effectively, further empowering them to save lives. By enabling bystanders to control bleeding, these kits can help reduce the burden on emergency medical services, allowing them to focus on more critical cases.

The rise in school shootings has highlighted the critical need for effective bleeding control measures in educational institutions, making bleed control kits an essential tool for ensuring the safety and well-being of students and staff members. Having bleed control kits readily available can significantly enhance the overall safety and preparedness of a school environment, giving staff and students a sense of security and confidence.

Epi Pens

A significant percentage of anaphylactic reactions in schools occur in students with no known allergies, highlighting the need for readily available epinephrine. Approximately 8% of children have food allergies, and 18% of children with food allergies will have a reaction at school.

Anaphylaxis can occur in students with no known allergies, and even in those with known allergies who may not have access to their personal epinephrine auto-injectors. Epinephrine is the primary treatment for anaphylaxis, and prompt administration can be lifesaving.

School-stocked epinephrine auto-injectors, like EpiPens, are crucial for treating life-threatening allergic reactions (anaphylaxis), especially for students with undiagnosed or poorly managed allergies, providing a safety net for all students.

Stocked epinephrine is a safety net for students who may have an allergic reaction and don't have their own epinephrine auto-injector, or for students with a confirmed allergy who may not have access to their EAIs or may need additional doses.

Schools should have trained staff (like nurses) who are prepared to administer epinephrine and recognize the signs of anaphylaxis. Programs like EpiPen4Schools aim to provide schools with access to epinephrine auto-injectors at no cost, making it easier for schools to be prepared.

Many states have laws that allow or mandate schools to stock epinephrine and provide legal protection for staff who administer it. Failure to properly recognize and treat anaphylaxis has led to fatalities in schools, emphasizing the importance of readily available epinephrine and trained staff.

Anti-Choking Devices

Foreign Body Airway Obstruction (FBAO) is a serious concern. FBAO, or choking, is a leading cause of accidental death in children. Having anti-choking devices in schools is crucial because they can be a lifesaver in choking emergencies, especially when traditional methods like the Heimlich maneuver prove ineffective. These devices provide an additional tool for school staff to quickly and effectively clear a child's airway, potentially preventing serious injury or death.

Using traditional methods such as the Heimlich maneuver may not always be enough, especially when considering that most people do not know how to properly do the Heimlich maneuver in the first place. In addition, the Heimlich maneuver and back blows are standard first aid procedures and they are not always successful in dislodging a foreign object.

In a choking emergency, every second counts, and having an anti-choking device readily available can make a critical difference. Devices, like the LifeVac, are designed to create suction to remove the obstruction. Schools should equip their staff with these devices and provide training on their proper use. Schools should also implement measures to prevent choking incidents, such as regular inspections of classrooms and play areas for potential hazards.

While anti-choking devices are gaining popularity, it's important to note that the FDA does not endorse them as a primary method of treatment and recommends following established choking rescue protocols first. Some states and local governments are considering legislation to mandate the presence of anti-choking devices in schools.

Naloxone "Narcan"

Naloxone is a medication designed to quickly reverse the effects of an opioid overdose. It works by binding to opioid receptors in the brain, effectively blocking the effects of drugs like heroin and prescription painkillers.

In 2023, The U.S. Food and Drug Administration gave nationwide approval for nonprescription naloxone nasal spray, also known by brand names such as Narcan® or RiVive®.

The nasal spray form of naloxone is available over the counter (OTC) for use in the emergency treatment of a known or suspected opioid overdose. Other forms of naloxone with higher doses or different delivery systems are available by prescription only (National Institute on Drug Abuse [NIDA], 2022).

The opioid crisis has become a significant public health issue, elevating to a public health emergency in 2017, with rising numbers of overdoses affecting all segments of society, including school-aged children.

Statistics reveal the alarming impact of opioids on communities. According to the Centers for Disease Control and Prevention (CDC), opioid overdoses account for tens of thousands of deaths annually in the United States. According to data from the Centers for Disease Control and Prevention (CDC) an average of 22 adolescents died of drug overdoses every week in 2022 in the United States.

Schools are not immune to this crisis, with reports of opioid-related incidents occurring on school grounds. This reality has prompted some schools and school districts to consider stocking naloxone as a preventive measure.

In 2023, the White House Office of National Drug Control Policy Director and U.S. Secretary of Education jointly disseminated an official letter to educators stating that every school in the United States should maintain a supply of naloxone. In addition, this letter strongly advised that both school staff and students should be prepared to administer the lifesaving medication, in the event of a suspected overdose in school (Cardona & Gupta, 2023).

The Federal Substance Abuse and Mental Health Services Administration (SAMHSA, 2023) has also recommended that every school, including elementary schools, should have naloxone readily available on-site to reduce overdose fatalities. Though schools may choose which form(s) of naloxone to use, school nursing knowledge is vital to guide medication administration decision-making.

While each state determines its own legislative and regulatory policies pertaining to medication administration and school nursing services in schools, all states have some form of law regarding the access to naloxone (Legislative Analysis and Public

Medical Equipment

Policy Association [LAPPA], 2022). It is critical that states respond to calls from federal agencies to provide naloxone in schools.

School nurses have the skills to provide and oversee emergency medication and treatments using albuterol inhalers, epinephrine, glucagon, and automated external defibrillators. Adding access to naloxone in schools is one more way to protect students and members of the school community from a life-threatening condition (McDonald et al., 2020).

Any person, with or without training, may administer OTC naloxone nasal spray according to directions on the package labeling (FDA, 2023; SAMHSA, 2023). Administering naloxone is straightforward, often involving a nasal spray that is easy to use with minimal training. Many school districts that have implemented naloxone programs report successful outcomes with manageable training requirements.

However, the presence of a school nurse in every school all day is the best practice for the safe management and oversight of medication administration in school, whether the medication is prescription or OTC (Butler et al., 2020; Lowe et al., 2022).

Additionally, school nurses can offer valuable education that helps staff and students recognize the signs of a potential opioid overdose and familiarizes individuals with proper naloxone administration procedures. As a part of overdose response training, school nurses can emphasize the need for essential actions to call 911 for transport to an emergency department and to deliver rescue breaths for abnormal or absent respirations (LAPPA, 2021).

All schools should have written emergency plans to address suspected opioid overdose, as part of emergency preparedness and response protocols, procedures, and policies. School nurses are key contributors to the evidence-based development of this harm reduction planning (Readiness and Emergency Management for Schools [REMS] Technical Assistance [TA] Center, 2023).

School nursing expertise and collaboration are crucial for planning, coordinating, and implementing evidence-based emergency preparedness and response actions and essential healthcare for opioid overdose. These interventions include ensuring the availability and access to naloxone in every school to protect the lives of each student and member of the school community.

Preparedness is paramount in emergencies. Training can cover a range of scenarios, from active shooter situations to natural disasters, preparing staff for a variety of potential emergencies.

A properly trained staff can respond quickly and appropriately, potentially saving lives during medical emergencies, natural disasters, or acts of violence. Training ensures that staff know how to implement emergency protocols, use safety equipment (like fire extinguishers), and follow established procedures for evacuations, lockdowns, and shelter-in-place situations.

Having clearly identified response procedures, and training will instill confidence and reduce the likelihood of panic, allowing for a more organized and effective response. When staff members are trained, they feel more capable and confident in their ability to handle emergencies, which can be crucial during stressful situations.

Drills and Exercises

Many jurisdictions require specific emergency response training for schools, making it a necessary part of maintaining compliance. The Federal Emergency Management Agency (FEMA) through the Homeland Security Exercise Evaluation Program (HSEEP) defines each type of training activity in the following manner:

Exercise:
An exercise is an instrument to train for, assess, practice, and improve performance in prevention, protection, response, and recovery capabilities in a risk-free environment. Exercises can be used for:

- Testing and validating policies, plans, procedures, training, equipment, and interagency agreements
- Clarifying and training personnel in roles and responsibilities
- Improving interagency coordination and communications
- Identifying gaps in resources
- Improving individual performance
- Identifying opportunities for improvement (essentially all training)

Exercises can be classified into two broad categories: discussion-based and operations-based.

Discussion-Based Exercise:
This type of exercise typically highlights existing plans, policies, mutual-aid agreements, and procedures, and can be used as tools to familiarize agencies and personnel with current or expected capabilities. Discussion-based exercises include seminars, workshops, tabletops, and games.

Operations-Based Exercise:
Operations-based exercises are characterized by actual response, mobilization of apparatus and resources, and commitment of personnel, usually held over an extended period of time. Operations-based exercises can be used to validate plans, policies, agree-

ments, and procedures and include drills, functional exercises, and full-scale exercises.

They can clarify roles and responsibilities, identify gaps in resources needed to implement plans and procedures, and improve individual and team performance.

It's important to first identify the different Operations-Based Exercise Examples shown below:

Drill:
A drill is a coordinated, supervised activity usually employed to test a single, specific operation or function within a single entity. Drills are commonly used to provide training on new equipment, develop or test new policies or procedures, or practice and maintain current skills.

Prior to conducting any drill it's important to take into consideration the aspects of developmental and mental health and the impact and effect that certain drills can have on your students, especially those with special needs.

The behavior of an adult in an emergency directly affects the physical and psychological safety of students in crisis. Therefore, the effectiveness of any drill relies on educating and training adults carefully, responsibly, and continually. Students view faculty and staff as the designated trusted adults on site and look to them for direction and guidance. When adults are well-trained and stay calm, the students are more likely to follow and gain confidence and ability.

Drills may lead to stressful or traumatic reactions. If the drill involves sensorial experience, then participation should never be mandated for staff or students. Staff should also be taught to recognize common trauma reactions to help identify when students, fellow staff members, or they need to be removed from the drill. Additionally, drills should be conducted early enough in the day to allow for debriefing participants afterward and assessing any adverse reaction.

Educators should monitor the reactions of themselves, each other, and students during the drill and have a means to quickly notify drill coordinators if a person exhibits physical (e.g., asthma or panic attack) or emotional (e.g., hysterical) reactions. Such reactions would necessitate removal from the drill and immediate medical support. School-employed health and mental health professionals must be present during the drill and available for assistance.

Emotional or physical reactions can be delayed following a highly intense simulation drill. School staff and students should have access to school-employed mental health professionals after the event to provide additional assistance if needed.

Active Shooter / Lockdown drills must always be announced days if not more in advance and disclosed to all participants as there is too much risk for students and staff to believe an unannounced drill is real, causing unnecessary fear or strong physical reactions to defend oneself.

Coordination should also be made with neighbors and/or the community particularly if the drill will include the use of the exterior of your school buildings and involve off campus evacuation sites.

Training

Emergency preparedness drills are practiced to prepare people for an emergency. Schools should prepare an annual schedule of all drills that will be performed for a full 12-month calendar. The drill schedule should be all hazard based and cover the full spectrum of lockdown, evacuation and shelter. It is very important that the school conduct safety drills throughout the school year to ensure students and staff/faculty are well-prepared in the event of an emergency.

It is recommended that your school has the goal of achieving at least one drill per month during the school year and summer months. These drills should be followed by an internal debrief and After-Action Report (AAR) identifying strengths and areas of improvement required.

Additional drills should be added throughout the year. Drills and exercises should be structured in a way that allows for practice in decision making. These types of scenarios serve to make it clear to school staff that they are not only authorized to take immediate action but are expected to do so.

Have a school employee pull the fire alarm (only if you have put the fire detection system in test mode and notified the monitoring company prior to the drill to eliminate the potential for a false alarm and unnecessary emergency responder activation), ask them where the nearest AED is located, block a stairwell during a building evacuation, have them list two possible locations off-campus that could be used as a rallying point if they suddenly had to direct students away from the campus.

Such activities should not be used to expose a staff member's lack of ability or knowledge. But rather, any incorrect response or action should be immediately corrected, and the participants should leave with the knowledge that they are better prepared to handle an incident than they were before the exercise. This type of activity is empowering for faculty and staff members.

Drill Frequency:

- Evacuation Drills (Fire drill frequency based on your local and state requirements)
- Shelter in Place Drills (A minimum of twice per school year)
- Active Shooter drills (A minimum of twice per school year. Always announced in advance)

Recommendations include:

- Visitors are accounted for during drills.
- There are written standards setting expectations of each emergency team member for each type of drill.
- Individuals with disabilities are accommodated during the drill.
- After action reviews are held following each exercise/drill or emergency.
- Developing corrective action plans based on the findings of the after-action reviews.

At the beginning of the school year, or prior to any drill, staff should be given specific instructions regarding:

- The type, purpose, and objective of the drill, including possible scenarios when each action response would be appropriate.
- Their roles and the specific behavior(s) they are expected to display.

- Specific details of evacuation routes, safe assembly areas, safe spots in each classroom for each type of drill, etc.
- Special instructions and provisions for individuals with special needs.
- Talking points for students during the drill that are specific to the drill at hand.
- Procedures for staff feedback as a part of the evaluation process of every drill.

Prior to each drill, students should be given specific instructions in a developmentally (age appropriate) language regarding:

- A review about the importance of emergency drills
- The type, purpose and objective of the drill, i.e., to evacuate the building should there be a fire or other reason the building is deemed unsafe
- Their roles and the specific behavior(s) they are expected to display, e.g., walking silently in single file, how to duck and cover for a tornado
- A review of the checklist of action responses in creating the directions to be given for who should do what and to what standard
- An explanation as to why they may not be told exactly what has prompted the drill or call for emergency action responses
- Special provisions for individuals with special needs

Functional Exercise (FE):
A functional exercise examines and/or validates the coordination, command, and control between multi-agency coordination centers. A functional exercise includes simulated deployment of

resources and personnel, rapid problem solving, and a highly stressful environment.

Full-Scale Exercise (FSE):
A full-scale exercise is a multi-agency, multi-jurisdictional, multi-discipline exercise involving functional and "boots on the ground" response.

Employee Training

People often envision security as a physical, tangible item, such as a gate or fence, or security cameras. In reality, the first, and best line of defense is an alert, well-trained staff. Developing and practicing crisis management plans and life safety procedures protects students, staff, faculty, school property and brand reputation. In emergency management circles, hope is not a strategy.

The development of a School Emergency Operations Plan (SEOP) is only one component of school emergency preparedness. Plans are only as effective as those who implement them. To effectively implement a plan and its emergency procedures, the school must train their employees. Annual staff training is a critical component to every school's emergency preparedness to ensure that school staff members are prepared to handle a crisis if one occurs.

Nothing is more valuable to the safety and security of a school than a well-trained faculty and staff. Whether it is through an orientation to a particular aspect of the school's emergency plans, a staff-initiated drill, or a full-scale exercise; providing on-going training is the most significant way to increase the security posture of the school community.

Training

The United States Marine Corps defines situational awareness as the knowledge and understanding of the current situation that promotes a timely, relevant, and accurate assessment in order to facilitate decision making (Department of the Navy, 2011). Situational awareness is a learned skill that can give school officials the ability to make critical decisions based on often limited information.

All administrators, faculty and staff, including bus drivers, cafeteria workers, janitors, office staff, and specialty staff should be educated regarding the overall emergency procedures for the school or campus, outlining roles and responsibilities for all parties.

Procedures should be put in place for educating substitute teachers and newly hired staff. Everyone should be provided with written instructions on drilling procedures and educated about the importance of emergency drills. Time should be allocated for staff to ask questions and provide feedback.

Emergency Procedure Response Training

This training should be conducted on an annual basis before every opening day for all faculty, staff members and new hires. This training should review all emergency procedures such as lockdown, evacuation and shelter in place as well as discuss evacuating the disabled, and on campus and off campus evacuation sites.

Active Shooter Response Training

This training should be conducted on an annual basis for all faculty, staff members and new hires. This training should include an option-based response (Run Hide Fight) overview as well as scenario-based exercises that will allow your staff the ability to walk through the survival strategies of an active shooter situation. These scenarios should include assessing the attacker's location, building barricades, fortifying door hardware, and the elements of taking back control of an attacker. It is highly recommended that this training be facilitated by an experienced instructor who has a proven track record and can provide school references.

Behavioral Threat Assessment Team Training

This training should be conducted annually for the behavioral threat assessment team. This training should review the proper threat assessment process, policies, legal aspects, law enforcement intervention, screening forms that will be used and include a tabletop exercise developed to practice the assessment of a credible threat.

Incident Command Team (ICT) Training

This training should be conducted for the Incident Command Team (ICT) every other year at a minimum to refresh participants on team structure, purpose and the duties assigned. This training should also include a tabletop exercise for the ICT to work through a crisis from start up to close down as well as recovery, mitigation and continuity of operations.

Training

Student Parent Reunification Team Training

This training should be conducted every other year at a minimum. This training should include an overview of the reunification procedures, team structure and duties assigned as well as making sure that the reunification kit/kits are properly maintained with current student rosters, student release forms as well as all other essential reunification kit items. It is also recommended that a Mach reunification site be set up with the team during this training to refresh exisiting team members and tarin new team members on site set up, flow and logistics.

CPR, AED, and First Aid Training

All these training courses should be offered and conducted annually for nurses, athletics staff, and coaches at a minimum. Ideally each training should be offered to as many employees that wish to participate.

Stop the Bleed

This training should be conducted every year for nurses, athletics staff, and coaches at a minimum. Ideally this training should be offered to as many employees that wish to participate. Most STOP THE BLEED® courses last no more than 90 minutes. A typical Stop the Bleed training course will include a formal presentation that is followed by hands-on practice of applying direct pressure, packing a wound, and using a tourniquet to stop bleeding.

In Summary

Training school staff in all aspects of emergency response is crucial for creating a safe and secure learning environment. It equips them with the knowledge and skills to handle various emergencies effectively, minimizing panic and maximizing the chances of positive outcomes for students and staff members.

Training is a long-term investment that benefits the entire school community by fostering a culture of preparedness and resilience. Engaging with local agencies and organizations through training can enhance the school's overall preparedness and response capabilities.

About the Author

Bradd Atkinson is a retired Baltimore County Police Officer. After retiring from Law Enforcement, he embarked on the private security sector in various leadership roles for several National Companies ranging from Vice President to Director level positions where he oversaw statewide security operations with large multi-million-dollar budgets, city business districts as well as Public and Independent School Safety and Security programs.

He has written and conducted countless Security Best Practice workshops for Schools, House of Worship Leadership, Licensed Security Personnel, and National Corporations. He has also written and developed community policing models and advanced school security training programs for college police departments and K-12 school security programs, many of whom also have on campus daycare centers.

He has served teams such as the Operation Delaware Counter Terrorism Organization and the International Cargo Security Council where he played an instrumental part in crime prevention, anti-terrorism measures and risk management. He has also been a licensed Security Agency Owner as well as a licensed Private Detective.

He has received extensive training from FEMA, DHS, NFPA and other organizations in National Incident Management System

(NIMS), Incident Command Systems (ICS), Mass Casualty Incidents, Emergency Management and Preparedness for Schools and Houses of Worship, Diversity Awareness, Cargo Security, Target Hardening, Characteristics of Armed Subjects, Counter Terrorism, Workplace Violence, Background Investigation, Visitor Management and Close Quarters Defense (CQD). He is also trained in Behavioral Threat Assessment and is a Certified School Resource Officer through the National Association of School Resource Officers N.A.S.R.O.

He is an Active Shooter/Hostile Event Response Program Specialist through NFPA 3000, and a Certified Active Shooter Response Instructor who utilizes the Run, Hide, Fight model. To date he has trained over 20,000 individuals in Active Shooter Response.

He has also been trained in Crime Prevention through Environmental Design (CPTED) and has worked with architects to improve target hardening designs. He is experienced with Surveillance Camera Systems and Access Control Systems and is a certified AMAG Access Control Operator.

In 2016/2017 he was awarded the Security Director of the Year Award from the Maryland Center for School Safety for his dedication and commitment to the Independent School community. He has presented at National Conferences on how to effectively implement an option-based response active shooter response protocol.

He has a combined 30 plus years of law enforcement and private security experience. He has provided services to high level national-level clients including DuPont, Bank of America, Chrysler, Honeywell, Valero Fuel, and Legg Mason.

He has worked with major city business districts such as Harbor East in Baltimore Maryland with the development and implementation of their physical security programs to include command centers, surveillance cameras, access control systems and armed and unarmed security guard programs.

He has written, developed and continues to deliver numerous training programs to his clients to include Emergency Procedure Response, Identify Report Prevent, Active Shooter Response, Campus Watch Team, Incident Command Team, and Student Parent Reunification.

His most recent development is the Identify Report Prevent protocol which teaches participants to identify risk factors, warning signs, and pre-attack indicators which can all be precursors to violent acts and to recognize them to increase the chances of preventing a violent act from occurring. This training is used as a precursor to his Active Shooter Response Training program.

He has provided all levels of his services and support to countless independent schools, public school districts, corporate level clients and large houses of worship. He has also helped independent schools implement armed security guard programs to include daily operating procedures and high-level armed response training programs in a school environment.

He is well known for his high level of organizational professionalism, commitment to his clients, consistent methods to effectively conduct assessments, develop and implement plans and procedures, and his ability to conduct training programs that empower his clients to confidently respond to crisis situations.

For inquiries contact the author at:
www.riskmitigationllc.com